GERMAN PERSPECTIVES

GERMAN PERSPECTIVES

Essays on German Literature

BY

R. HINTON THOMAS, M.A.

Joint-author of *Expressionism in German Life, Literature and the Theatre (1910-1924)* and author of *The Classical Ideal in German Literature*

CAMBRIDGE

W. HEFFER AND SONS LTD

1940

M. A. T.

In memoriam

Printed and Bound in Great Britain at the Works of
W. HEFFER & SONS LTD., CAMBRIDGE, ENGLAND

PREFACE

My primary reason for publishing this volume is a personal one. The essays here represented were written so directly under the inspiration of my mother that I felt at her death that it would be a fitting memorial to her if they were allowed to appear under one cover.

Six of these papers have already appeared in various journals. Chapter I was composed as a lecture which was delivered to the English Goethe Society at King's College, London, in May 1938 and was published in the *Publications of the English Goethe Society* in 1939. As far as I am aware, it constitutes the first attempt to define the nature of Goethe's rôle and influence in the long procession of literary movements which reflect the uneasy course of German thought during the present ill-starred century. Its conclusions, I fear, are not encouraging. Mere worship of past achievement, it is true, does not necessarily connote spiritual health, but arrogant aloofness with regard to her greatest poet, whose prestige is challenged nowhere else in Europe, is surely an indication of the rapid deterioration of the German mind in recent years. Of the literary movements outlined in this introductory essay, that generally known as expressionism strikes our less effulgent and more temperate Anglo-Saxon mind as the most peculiar. Nevertheless, I have been able to collect some evidence—and much more could have been mustered if space had permitted it—in Chapter II (completed just before the outbreak of the present conflict and here published for the first time) to indicate some respects in which the expressionist theatre in Germany has fertilised our own dramatic work. When in 1939 I published, in collaboration with Dr. Richard Samuel, my book on *Expressionism in German Life, Literature and the Theatre (1910–1924)*, Mr. Stephen Spender was prompted to deny, in the *London Mercury*, his alleged kinship with the movement. In this chapter I have extended the allegation to his dramatic work, and I imagine that he will be no less aroused (and probably no more convinced) by this further *recherche de la paternité*. Chapter III was the outcome of some research undertaken in Switzerland in preparation for the book mentioned above; it appeared in the *Modern Language Review*, July, 1937. Chapter IV is reprinted from that book. I have also taken from the same source some paragraphs on the Danish philosopher Sören Kierkegaard, which I have added to an article which appeared in *German Life and Letters* in October 1937 under the title "Franz Kafka and the Religious Aspect of Expressionism." I trust therefore that Chapter V will be of interest, not only in view of the considerable attention that the work of Kafka has awakened latterly in this country but also as it shows that ideas akin to those of Barthian theology can be traced also in the more general field of German culture. This question awaits a closer investigation which, I feel, it would amply repay. The last two chapters take us into spheres which there is a temptation to regard as much more stable and secure in their spiritual values than those dealt with in the foregoing essays. This would, however, be a misleading impression, for one is concerned with poetry reflecting the tortured soul of modern Austria, while the other gives an account of an early appreciation of the wild genius of Beethoven by a man who, disgusted and bewildered by his age, fell a prey to madness. Of these two papers, Chapter VI appeared in *German Life and Letters*, July 1939, and was the fruit of a friendship formed before the wave of *Machtpolitik* overran Austria. Chapter VII appeared in *Music and Letters*. To the various authorities who kindly allowed me to make use of articles already published I wish here to express my gratitude.

R. H. T.

At Repton, Derby.
March, 1940.

CONTENTS

Chapter I
GOETHE IN THE LITERARY MOVE-MENTS OF THE TWENTIETH CENTURY

WRITING early in the century Hermann Bahr referred to the deep debt in which the poetry and thought of that day stood to Goethe who, he maintained, had become "der grosse Wegweiser, an dem jeder sich erst zu sich selbst findet."[1] In 1911 the same critic claimed that all poets since Goethe are contained in Goethe,[2] and asserted that we act in the true tradition of Goethe's thought when we approach his work subjectively and accept his ideas in the light of the special purposes of our own time.

It would, however, be misleading to assume that, from the beginning of this century, Goethe has always to this high degree been the philosopher and friend of German poets. It is the task of this paper to summarise the vicissitudes of fortune through which Goethe's reputation and influence have passed during the successive literary movements of the twentieth century, from naturalism to the present day.

The naturalists were divided in their attitude to Goethe. Some rejected him without reservation. One critic of the period, who was closely in sympathy with the movement, maintained that Karl Bleibtreu's manifesto *Die Revolution in der Literatur* (1885) was an ultimatum directed against Goethe.[3] Eugen Dühring's attack on *Die Grössen der Modernen Literatur* (1893) included Goethe, and Hermann Conradi shared with the hero of his novel *Phrasen* the contempt for "den edlen Landsmann der Rothschilds."[4]

On the other hand, there were naturalists whose impatience with tradition and convention led them to speak

[1] *Essays*, Leipzig, 1912.   [2] *Der Strom*, I, i.
[3] Leo Berg, "Goethe und unsere Zeit" in *Neue Essays*, 1909.
[4] Cf. *Lit. Echo*, I, 22.

1

with warm approval of the young Goethe. Characteristic of this view was the periodical of Heinrich and Julius Hart, the *Deutsche Monatsblätter*, where it is claimed that in the works of Goethe's Storm and Stress years "die entfesselten Geister des Volkes jauchzten, die Menschheit die Sprache wiederfand." In the essay "Für und gegen Zola," in the *Kritische Waffengänge*, naturalism is defined as the opposite of mere formalism which "durch Goethe, den Dichter der *Iphigenie*, unserer Literatur eingeimpft wurde." This must now be superseded by the "Naturalismus des Genies" and hence: "Wir müssen wieder anknüpfen an den jungen Goethe, den Schöpfer des *Werther* und *Faust*." In contrast to this emphasis on the vitality of Goethe's early works those of his later years are sometimes depreciated, as in Hartleben's *Goethe-Brevier* (1895), and Bierbaum speaks cynically of Goethe as a "Kunstgreis und Geheimrat."

Naturalism lingered on into the twentieth century, and it is noteworthy that, at the outset of our period, Wilhelm Bölsche, who in his *Naturwissenschaftliche Grundlagen der Poesie* (1887) had formulated the naturalist conception of the scientific basis of literature, attempted to justify these ideas by reference to Goethe. Thus, in his *Das Liebesleben in der Natur* (1900) he discusses and praises *Die Wahlverwandtschaften* in the light of scientific knowledge. In 1913 Goethe's poem *Selige Sehnsucht* furnished the motto and title for his *Stirb und Werde: Naturwissenschaftliche und kulturelle Plaudereien*, but it is in his lecture delivered at the Goethe celebrations at Frankfurt in 1899 and published in 1903, *Goethe im 20. Jahrhundert*, that we find his most representative naturalist interpretation of Goethe.

Bölsche's naturalist faith in the influence of *milieu* led him to the view that the traditional conception of guilt in the life of man was no longer valid, and it is from this standpoint that he discusses Goethe's contribution to the century that had just opened. Goethe, he claims, despite occasional evidence to the contrary, such as Mignon's song *Ihr führt ins Leben uns hinein,* rejected the idea of guilt, protested against it in the Prometheus Ode, and anticipated the naturalists' belief in the higher idea of evolution. Thus in *Faust* we have "den grössten Protest gegen den alten Schuldgedanken," for Faust's redemption through his striving is "der Triumph der Entwicklung." His conclusion is that we must abandon the historical conception of Goethe and re-create his spirit within ourselves in accordance with our own development. Thereby mankind will overcome the duality of existence and, when this is achieved, Goethe will according to the law of evolution be forgotten "weil wir alle Goethe sind."

We realise from Bölsche's arguments that naturalism felt a kinship with the monistic element in the scientific studies of the mature Goethe. A parallel kinship can be recognised in a group of ⸀mpressionist writers represented notably by Dehmel and Liliencron. Their attitude differs from the cool observation of nature of the naturalists and the negative receptivity of many neo-romantics by reason of their exuberant affirmation of the positive values of life.[1]

For Liliencron Goethe's supreme characteristic was the essential healthiness of his spiritual make-up:

> Jeder wirkliche Dichter
> Hat einen Stich ins Krankhafte;
> Du, Grösster,
> Warst ganz gesund.[2]

In contrast to Christ, Goethe symbolises in his mind man's desire to live life proudly and to the full:

> Oh, habe Dank, du Ewiger, jede Stunde:
> Du hast uns Hoheit über Tod und Leben
> Mit deiner selbstbewussten Stirn gegeben![3]

In his essay *Der Olympier Goethe* Dehmel gives us a picture of the "titanic genius" who "aus einem chaotischen Nebelbrodem von Schmerzen, Leidenschaften

---

[1] To this group the term "Lebensbejaher" has been applied. Cf. Elisabeth Darge, *Lebensbejahung in der deutschen Dichtung um 1900,* Breslau, 1934.

[2] *Ges. Werke,* II, p. 207.   [3] *Ibid.,* p. 284.

und Zweifeln . . . einen Kosmos herauszuläutern sucht." The divergence between this group and the naturalists is summed up by Liliencron in the poem *An Goethe* when he writes of him:

> Dich lieben sie nicht,
> Weil du zu frisch, zu natürlich,
> Zu wahr und offen bist.[1]

These are qualities dear to the hearts of these "Lebens-bejaher" and stand close to the aspirations of neo-romanticism in some of its aspects.

In 1899 appeared Rudolf Huch's *Mehr Goethe*, in which this neo-romantic attacked the narrowness of the naturalist view of literature, and demanded that poetry should abandon trivialities and re-establish the breadth of style that it had lacked since Goethe. This plea for a return to Goethe is mirrored also in the attitude to Goethe of Reinhard Johannes Sorge in his neo-romantic years. On the one hand, his enthusiasm was part of the neo-romantic cult of the past, and it is characteristic that his attention was directed especially to the later Goethe at the time of his association with Dornburg.[2] On the other, his veneration for Goethe was derived from the neo-romantic craving for a serene and untroubled beauty. Thus in his diary he notes: "Ruhe und Sicherheit im Verhältnis zu den Menschen. Goethes Einfluss," and a letter of 1910 contains the observation: "Das Ringen der Menschheit geht darauf hin, die Wirklichkeit schön zu leben, nicht schön zu träumen . . . Goethe hat es uns wieder und wieder gewiesen."[3]

The pre-occupation of the neo-romantics with Goethe was so absorbing that justice cannot be done to it in a résumé such as this. Only passing reference can be made to Albrecht Schaeffer's emphasis, in his volume of essays,

---

[1] *Ges. Werke*, I, p. 170.
[2] Cf. the poem *Dornburg* in *Der Jüngling. Die frühen Dichtungen*, München, 1925, p. 161.
[3] Cf. Martin Rockenbach, *Reinhard Johannes Sorge*, Leipzig, n.d., pp. 27–8.

Dichtung und Dichter,[1] on Goethe's "ursprüngliche Lebendigkeit," and his description of him as "der erste wirkliche Dichter des Seins." Schaeffer speaks also in the neo-romantic tradition when, in contrasting Goethe's poetry with that of Mörike, he stresses Goethe's oneness with nature, and when he interprets Iphigenia's longing to leave Tauris as the gothic yearning for infinity. Neo-romantic also is Thomas Mann's early short story *Schwere Stunde*,[2] in which he makes use of his favourite theme of the heroism that can emanate from weakness by contrasting Goethe and Schiller. No less characteristic is Richard Schaukal's claim, in his *Giorgione oder Gespräche über die Kunst* (1907), that Goethe's greatness lay partly in the fact that, unlike Schiller, his emotional experiences had "absolute" value, and that his emotional life was sufficiently rich to merit the epithet "dynamic." Only occasionally do we find in neo-romanticism criticism of Goethe, although Hofmannsthal contrasts the imaginative splendour of the poetry of D'Annunzio with what he regards as the shallow experiences that underlay the *Römische Elegien*, and speaks cynically of Goethe's "weise Beschränkung."[3] Likewise Max Dauthendey finds in *Faust* a lack of virile and direct impressions.[4] More typical, however, than these criticisms is Ricarda Huch's search for a new religion linked up with Goethe's thought and formulated in her *Entpersönlichung* (1922).[5]

Neo-romanticism was by its nature irrational, and it is therefore not surprising that both Dehmel and Liliencron, who in many aspects of their work must be regarded as

[1] Leipzig, 1923.

[2] Published in *Meister der modernen Erzählungskunst*, Berlin, n.d.

[3] *Loris. Die Prosa des jungen Hugo von Hofmannsthal*, Berlin, 1930, p. 106.

[4] Cf. *Weltall*, published however only in Danish with the title *Verdensaltet. Det nye sublime i Kunsten*, Copenhagen, 1893. Cf. H. G. Wendt, *Max Dauthendey. Poet-Philosopher*, New York, 1936, p. 99.

[5] For an account of this work cf. *Ricarda Huch. Persönlichkeit und Werk in Darstellungen ihrer Freunde*, Berlin, n.d., pp. 155 ff.

B

neo-romantics, borrow for their idea of poetry the authority of Goethe's remark to Eckermann: "Je inkommensurabler und für den Verstand unfassbarer eine poetische Produktion, desto besser." Dehmel uses Goethe's statement to support his own *Offenherzige Erklärung* (1908), and Liliencron's poem *An Otto Julius Bierbaum* is prefaced by a long quotation from the Conversations with Eckermann, in which Goethe exhorts writers to have the courage to surrender themselves to impressions and warns them against the danger of using poetry merely as the vehicle of abstractions. Goethe refers to his own poetry in which he sought to reproduce "Eindrücke sinnlicher, lebensfroher, lieblicher, bunter, hundertfältiger Art." Accordingly Liliencron wishes to impart to German poetry more of the naturalness of Goethe:

> Könnt ich unsern guten Deutschen
> Täglich eine Stunde Goethen
> Auf den Weg zum Tage geben:
> Ach, der Landsmann, immer, ewig
> Will und wünscht er nur Abstraktes.[1]

It is, above all, this sensuous aspect of Goethe's work that appeals to the neo-romantics. Thus, in Goethe's early poem *Königlich Gebet*, Hofmannsthal finds "diese blühende Wärme in sich"[2] which for the neo-romantic is the criterion of authentic poetry, and he praises in Goethe "die sinnliche Schönheit seiner Form"[3] which links his genius to that of Mozart. With this power of creating sense-impressions was combined in Goethe, so Hofmannsthal claims,[4] the power to awaken objects to life by allowing them to pass through his mind and be mirrored therein. Here we find perhaps the most characteristic neo-romantic interpretation of Goethe: "Denn dazu, glaube ich, sind Künstler: dass alle Dinge, die durch ihre Seele hindurchgehen, einen Sinn und eine Seele empfangen. 'Die Natur wollte wissen, wie sie

[1] In the section "Nebel und Sonne" in *Ges. Werke*, III.
[2] *Loris*, pp. 103 ff.   [3] *Ibid.*, p. 224.   [4] *Ibid.*, p. 235.

aussah, und schuf sich Goethe.' Und Goethes Seele hat wiederspiegelnd tausend Dinge zum Leben erlöst." Typical, also, in another passage[1] is the definition of the nature of Goethe's poetry as the "Seligkeit des Augenblicks" and the description of the poem *Selige Sehnsucht* as one of the "Landschaften der Seele."[2]

Fundamental to neo-romanticism is the conception of the festive element immanent throughout God's creation.[3] In an essay entitled *Goethes Opern und Singspiele*[4] Hofmannsthal interprets this side of Goethe's work from the standpoint of this idea. With reference to Goethe's *Der Zauberflöte zweiter Teil* he maintains that Goethe's mind represents a continuous progress from festival to festival, and he even discovers elements of world-festivity, of "jenes unnennbar Feierlichen," in *Wilhelm Meister*. Wilhelm's discourse on life and work is, according to Hofmannsthal, arranged in the mode of a solemnity which lacks only music to disclose its full festive effect, and Wilhelm's life is unrolled as "ein wahrhaft musikalischer Festgedanke." Goethe, more than any other poet, observes the chain of festivity in the process of nature, and *Faust II* depicts symbolically nature's sublime festivals.

It is, however, not only in these several aspects that neo-romanticism reveals a lively interest in Goethe, for his influence extends to the whole field of its conception of culture. It has rightly been claimed[5] that a line leads from Goethe's idea of the true home of culture as an aesthetically minded aristocracy to Schaeffer's imposing novel *Helianth* (1920). Perhaps one explanation of the unsatisfactory inner structure of this work lies in the fact that the new problems of the neo-romantic period,

[1] *Ges. Werke*, III, p. 248.   [2] *Ibid.*, p. 250.

[3] An important exponent of this idea was Dauthendey. Cf. Wendt, *op. cit.*

[4] In the *Berührung der Sphären*.

[5] Werner Mahrholz, *Deutsche Literatur der Gegenwart*. Revised edition, Berlin, 1931, pp. 234 ff.

such as the rise of the proletariat and the reign of capitalism, had between neo-romanticism and the world of
Goethe fixed an unbridgeable gulf. The fact that the
neo-romantics looked back to Goethe in their attempt to
establish a cultural foundation of life is evident, not only
from such writers as Morgenstern who revered Goethe
as one of the "neue Götter,"[1] but also from such a work
as Rudolf Huch's novel *Talion*. The theme of this work
is the problem of co-ordinating culture and life. The hero
Dohlen is deeply versed in Goethe, but he repeatedly
finds that Goethe's precepts do not prove adequate to
the situations in which he finds himself. Thus he cannot,
in the light of the sufferings that he has brought upon
himself, accept Goethe's idea that all human failings are
atoned for by pure humanity. This novel shows the lack
of contact with reality which was the weakness of neo-
romanticism in general, a failing which is symbolised
at the close by Dohlen's passion for a lady who no longer
exists. The neo-romantic view of Goethe suffered from
this lack of reality. It was so subjective that it was in no
sense pregnant with real value and, by being in the first
place an aesthetic view, it overlooked the gap that
separated Goethe's world from that of neo-romanticism.
The admiration of the neo-romantics for Goethe was
sufficiently lively to colour their own work, but they lacked
the organic vitality necessary for the absorption of
Goethe's fundamental teaching.

The dissatisfaction with the naturalist view of life,
which found expression in the work of the neo-romantics,
was also the point of departure for those writers whom it
is usual to designate as neo-classical, and whose leader
was Paul Ernst. Neo-romanticism and neo-classicism are
terms that suggest mutual exclusion, and yet here as
everywhere *les extrèmes se touchent*. As far as their conception of Goethe is concerned, the point of contact
must be sought in Stefan George. The dual character

[1] Michael Bauer, *Christian Morgensterns Leben und Werk*, München,
1933, p. 98.

of George's view of Goethe[1] is seen in his anthology of Goethe's poems *Deutsche Dichtung II*. The choice of poems is significant; only those are selected for inclusion which contain "die tiefsten lebensgluten" but "in der schönsten bändigung." A similar combination of neo-romantic and neo-classical values is observed by comparing the two poems of George, *Goethe-Tag* and *Goethes letzte Nacht in Italien*. In the former the veil is lifted from the Olympian serenity of the classical Goethe to reveal the inner workings of his soul, his early struggles and his spiritual unrest. It is noteworthy, however, that in *Goethes letzte Nacht in Italien* George should have singled out as the subject of the poem the moment when Goethe left Italy enriched by his recognition of classical form.[2]

It is to the work of Paul Ernst that we must look to find what Goethe meant to the neo-classicists. Finding that neither the prosaic character of naturalism nor the ethereal ambitions of neo-romanticism corresponded to his idea of art, Ernst endeavoured to broaden the basis of literature by recalling it to the larger issues of tragedy and form. It is strange to observe that, in 1913, Ernst accused Goethe of lacking "den Willen zur Form." It was natural therefore, he says, that Goethe should have been attracted to the "Novelle" which offers the poet the advantage of a recipe.[3] It is a far cry from this

[1] George's view of Goethe is summed up by August Closs in his article "Georges Goethebild" in the *Germ. Rom. Monatshefte*, 1935.

[2] The link between the neo-romantic and the neo-classical conception of Goethe is found also in the *Wege nach Weimar* which appeared in serial form from 1905 and consisted of selections from eminent writers with original contributions and comments by Friedrich Lienhard. Here German literature is directed back to the home of Goethe so that it may re-orientate itself by contact with true culture, and the emphasis is laid on the works of Goethe's classical period. However, throughout, and especially in the introductory section *Was ist aesthetische Kultur?*, the stress on the aesthetic aspect of culture, on the "seelisches Erlebnis" and the "dekoratives Element" shows an unmistakable relationship to the world of neo-romanticism.

[3] Cf. the chapter "Zu Goethes Novellen und Märchen" in the *Tagebuch eines Dichters*, München, 1932.

disparaging conception to his essay on *Iphigenie* in *Der Weg zur Form*, in which Goethe's play is praised as the first step in the true dramatic tradition. Between these conflicting views lies that conception of Goethe and German classicism at which Ernst arrives, when he considers the social background of German literature in the eighteenth century.

In the *Zusammenbruch des deutschen Idealismus* (1919) Ernst divides social life into "organic" and "inorganic" phases. Characteristic of an inorganic stage is an inner instability in man. In such an age men become increasingly individualistic and, at the same time, are unable to bear the burden of individuality. In our own time, says Ernst, evidence of the inorganic character of the age is to be found in the existence of the proletariat. In the eighteenth century the "Bürgertum" corresponded to the proletariat and, in the work of Goethe, the inorganic element finds expression in the gap that separated art and life. German classicism was the manifestation of an ideal of life that did not exist, and already in *Werther* this cleavage, he believes, can be observed. German classicism was, therefore, by its very nature romantic and cannot for this reason be the basis of later thought, since true classicism can only be the product of an organic age. In the *Grundlagen der neuen Gesellschaft* (1930) Ernst makes it clear that the aim of the neo-classicists was not to link up with the ideals of Goethe, but to find something to take their place. "Daraus ergiebt sich unsere Aufgabe," he writes: "wir müssen etwas finden, das dem entspricht, das zur Zeit Lessings und Kants, Goethes und Schillers das Humanitätsideal war, ein Ziel für das Leben, einen Zweck für das Handeln."

Ernst's view of the true purpose of art and its relation to life contains obvious weaknesses, and the measure of effectiveness that he achieved in his own work does not invite the conclusion that his ideas will stand the test of time. Though at some points he apparently rejects the age of Goethe as a foundation for posterity, he never ceased to cherish the hope that a compromise might be found. Thus, in *Der Weg zur Form*, he believes that it may not be impossible to re-create in modern surroundings something corresponding to Weimar in the eighteenth century, since, in his view, all that Goethe achieved as a poet he owed to the inspiration of this community.[1] Despite Ernst's criticisms of the age and work of Goethe, the fact remains that neither he nor his fellow neo-classicists, such as Lublinski or Wilhelm von Scholz, succeeded either in precept or in practice in making the classical ideal more than an academic problem.

Neither neo-romanticism nor neo-classicism proved adequate for the sustained intellectual leadership of Germany and, in the years immediately preceding the War, a new group of writers came to the fore who were soon known as the expressionists. The main points in their programme were the need for a free outlet for the emotions and a radical break with tradition. We are not surprised that their dionysiac view of life led the expressionists to admiration of Kleist and Hölderlin, but it is strange that they neglected Goethe, whose early works corresponded in spirit and style to their own revolutionary ambitions.

The resemblance between the expressionists and the early Goethe is mirrored in the language. The expressionists aimed at giving the literary language greater elasticity by liberating it from the rules of syntax. It has been justly observed[2] that, if Goethe was entitled to claim that darkness peered out of the bushes "mit hundert schwarzen Augen," the expressionists had the right to

[1] A somewhat similar idea is found in Rudolf Pannwitz, the author of a number of neo-classical dramas and the leader of a circle of poets. In 1921 appeared his pamphlet *Aus dem Chaos zur Gemeinschaft* in which he describes the new community that he envisages, and which is to be "das tatgewordene ideal einer verantwortlichen gemeinschaft individualer aristokraten."

[2] F. J. Schneider, *Der expressive Mensch und die deutsche Lyrik der Gegenwart*, Stuttgart, 1927, p. 120.

maintain that they could "hear the silence." This affinity was overlooked by the expressionists, and it is surely remarkable that their only tribute to such a poem as *An Schwager Kronos*, which in its underlying spirit of restless activity so strikingly anticipates the style and spirit of expressionist poetry, is the musical setting of it by Herwarth Walden, the leader of the "Sturm" circle.

In 1916 appeared Hermann Bahr's book on expressionism in which he makes frequent reference to Goethe as a spiritual forefather of the movement. Hanns Johst, obviously irritated by this attempt to establish a precedent for a movement proud of its originality, admitted this resemblance, but denied in his review of Bahr's book[1] that it prejudiced the novelty of the cause. The year that witnessed this crossing of the swords of the two generations saw the appearance of Gundolf's biography of Goethe which, by its stress on the unity of Goethe's mind as a whole, by emphasising "sein transzendentales Ich"[2] and by applying Dilthey's "Erlebnistheorie,"[3] brought literary criticism into touch with the expressionist idea of the dynamic personality.

Expressionism as a whole, however, did not share Gundolf's sympathy with Goethe. Much more representative is Sternheim's virulent attack on Goethe in *Tasso oder Die Kunst des Juste Milieu* (1921).[4] Expressionism grew up under the influence of the War and was permeated by a feeling of moral responsibility for the welfare of mankind, and Sternheim takes Goethe to task for his supposed lack of interest towards his fellowmen. Goethe, therefore, "stand im Menschenerdreich nur auf einem Bein," and so Sternheim sets out to inter-

[1] In *Die Neue Rundschau*, May, 1916.

[2] Werner Mahrholz, *Literargeschichte und Literarwissenschaft*, Leipzig, 1932, pp. 110 ff.

[3] Rudolf Unger, "Wandlungen des literarischen Goethebildes seit 100 Jahren" in *Gesammelte Studien* 11, Berlin, 1929.

[4] Sternheim nevertheless begins his essay with a guarded tribute to Gundolf.

pret him "in anderem Sinn auf neue Art." As a true expressionist he rejects the idea that the aim of art is pleasure, and believes that its concern is morality. In his view art should bridge the gap between time and eternity and thereby make man conscious of his transcendental heritage. He sees German classicism as degraded by its narrow bourgeois outlook and ascribes to Kant the crime of having stressed the finite responsibilities of man at the expense of the infinite. From the same standpoint he rejects Goethe's "Vertiefung in Vorhandenes," which, he believes, put an end to the mystical tradition that had flourished since the Middle Ages. The decline of this mysticism inaugurated a sterilisation of the German spirit, symbolised by the substitution of "Erlaubt ist, was sich ziemt," for the more liberal doctrine of "Erlaubt ist, was gefällt."

Sternheim was not alone in failing to recognise that, in the work of the early Goethe, an authoritative precedent could be found for the dynamic moment of expressionist art. The same enthusiasm for gothic art that had inspired Goethe's essay on the Strassburg Minster in *Von deutscher Art und Kunst* led the early expressionist Ernst Stadler to make the cathedral the subject of his poem *Gratia Divinae pietatis*, and Walzel[1] has shown that the "Sturm und Drang" circle, and in particular writers such as Lenz and Klinger, were among the ancestors of expressionism. Yet Carl Einstein, in his *Brief über den Roman*,[2] speaks disparagingly of Goethe as being "in seinen Epen eher ein Verbreiter von Bildung und Einsicht als von Kunst," and, in the preface to the expressionist anthology *Expressionistische Dichtungen*, Herwarth Walden dismisses him as a misguided poet of ephemeral importance.

To this general hostility to Goethe among the expressionists must be added that of the activists who constitute a special group within the movement, and

[1] *Einführung in die Kunst der Gegenwart*, Leipzig, 1920, p. 45.
[2] *Anmerkungen*, 1916.

whose immediate concern was active participation in the welfare of men. Their influence reached its highest point in the year of the Russian Revolution, and their ideas were coloured by communism. To these activists Goethe was repellent by virtue of his alleged abstractness and passivity. Heinrich Mann, in his essay *Voltaire-Goethe*, contrasted the French writer with Goethe as pre-eminently a man of action, and a writer in the expressionist anthology *Die Erhebung*[1] accused Goethe of proud self-satisfaction, which rendered impossible any "soziologische Befreiung." Instead of being a saviour and a leader Goethe was a despot, who failed to realise that his own problem of the two souls within his breast was shared even by the lowest classes of society.

Despite the expressionists' criticism of Goethe no one can deny the strong influence—both formal and philosophical—of *Faust* upon the expressionist drama. The expressionists had revolted against the tendency of the neo-romantics to limit their outlook to the world of beauty, and they sought to introduce into literature the world of sordid and even prosaic reality. Since, however, they failed to find that fourth-dimensional world in which time and eternity meet, they were conscious of an inner duality, and, for the expression of this, they often had recourse to the duality Faust-Mephisto. Wedekind makes the heroine of his *Franziska* 1911 take a journey through the successive stages of life accompanied by the Mephistophelian figure of Veit Kunz. Another link with Goethe's play is furnished by Reinhard Johannes Sorge's dramatic dialogue *Kinder der Erde* 1908, of which the language alone is sufficient to indicate its indebtedness, and, in his main work, *Der Bettler*, the "Geist, der stets verneint" is found in the person of the Poet's Friend. It exists also in Kornfeld's *Himmel und Hölle* in Jakob, the "ewiger Protest," in Hasenclever's *Der Sohn*, and in a number of other expressionist dramas that include Csokor's *Der Grosse Kampf*, Friedrich Wolf's

[1] Adrien Turel, *Jedermanns Recht auf Genialität.*

Das Bist Du and Arnold Zweig's *Die Sendung Semaels*.[1] The most conspicuous reincarnation of the relationship between Mephistopheles and Faust is to be found in Werfel's *Der Spiegelmensch*. The subject of this "Magic Trilogy" is the division of the ego through

> die Spiegelwelt,
> Die uns die Fratze gegenüberstellt
> Der eigenen Person in jedem Wesen,
> Die Welt, von der die Wenigsten genesen.

The ending of the dual relationship of Thamal and his other self, the Monk, leads to the rebirth of the hero after his "false self" has been destroyed. Thus in Werfel's play Goethe's conception of the Mephistophelian character is transferred to existence as a whole.

There is another feature of *Faust* that was grafted by the expressionists into their own work, namely the Ascension Scene at the end of the Second Part. The impatience of the expressionists with finite existence, and their failure to find a means of co-ordinating it with the world of infinity, led them in their works boldly to break through the barriers of time. Thus it was common practice with them to introduce into the close of their dramas a scene in which the action is suddenly transferred to the world of infinity, but without Goethe's careful transition. Examples of this technique are furnished by Kaiser's *Bürger von Calais* which culminates in "die Erhebung des Getöteten," after he is released from the trammels of earthly life; by Fritz von Unruh's *Vor der Entscheidung*, where in the last scene the stage is widened to a symbolical representation of infinity, as the Faustian lines are sung:

> Beugen, beugen
> Das eigene Haupt!
> Neigen, neigen!
> Ganz ungeglaubt
> Greift uns allen, allen Seelen
> Glaubenskraft die Bruderhand.

---

[1] Cf. B. Diebold, *Anarchie im Drama*, 4th ed. Berlin, 1928, where further examples are given.

and by Kornfeld's *Himmel und Hölle* in which the closing song of Maria and Johanna, and the final assurance of salvation for all, almost constitute a plagiarism of *Faust II*. So also in *Der Spiegelmensch* the revelation of the "higher reality" takes place only after the stage has been transformed to represent "eine stark bewegte, trunkene Farben- und Formenwelt, die für den Zuschauer jene höhere Realität bedeuten soll."

A fundamental divergence, however, between Goethe and the expressionists lies in Goethe's close link with the "Bürgertum" of his time, and the expressionists' hatred of all that the term "bürgerlich" implies. At the same time as the expressionists were trying to free culture from its bourgeois associations, the attempt was being made by Thomas Mann to establish it upon a bourgeois foundation. Regarding Mann's interest in the poetical aspects of Goethe's work, he tells us[1] that it was only in his later years that he recognised the splendour of Goethe's style, and it is known[2] that before writing *Der Tod in Venedig* Mann steeped himself in *Die Wahlverwandtschaften*, in order to grasp the secret "dieses souveränen Stiles."

It is, however, the social factors which guided Goethe's mind that have most attracted Mann's interest. In the *Betrachtungen eines Unpolitischen* the chapter entitled *Bürgerlichkeit* is characteristically prefaced by Goethe's lines:

> Wo kam die schönste Bildung her,
> Und wenn sie nicht vom Bürger wär?

and in the *Brief an Hermann Grafen Keyserling* he answers the question "Was, im Grunde, bedeutet Bürgerlichkeit?" by reference to Wilhelm Meister's letter to Werner, in which he explains his love of the theatre as the longing of a man, conscious "seiner bürgerlich-unharmonischen Menschlichkeit," for correctness and perfection. The

---

[1] Cf. his note "Über Gottfried Keller" in *Rede und Antwort*.
[2] Cf. Otto Zarek's account of an interview with Mann in *Die Neue Rundschau*, June, 1925.

weakness of the "Bürgertum" lies, so Mann believes, in this lack of inner harmony and, since in Mann's view, Germany is the bourgeois country *par excellence*, it is incumbent upon Germans to seek the unity of soul and intellect. True culture, Mann continues, means the expression of a unified personality; it is "die Vergeistigung des Lebens und das Fleischwerden des Geistes, die Synthese von Seele und Geist."

Mann admires Goethe for having achieved this synthesis, and so, in *Goethe als Repräsentant des bürgerlichen Zeitalters*, he depicts him as the supreme example of "Lebensbürgerlichkeit," that is to say as the man who, undisturbed in the unity of mind and body, saw life steadily and saw it whole. Mann makes it clear that it would be mistaken to stress Goethe's love of order and tradition, his "Lebens ernstes Führen," at the expense of his high opinion of individual achievement. He points to Goethe's interest in the Renaissance as the "Epoche des erwachenden Individuums," and he finds this interest reflected in *Tasso* and the Life of Cellini. According to Mann this combination in Goethe of order and indivualism represents the highest type of "Bürgertum," and this alone can provide the basis for that true humanity which forms the subject of his catena of fragments *Goethe und Tolstoi*.

The year 1924 may be said to mark the abrupt end of expressionism. The spirit of orderliness re-entered German literature, supported by a reaction against the abstract tendencies of expressionism, and in 1926 appeared Eugen Diesel's *Weg durch das Wirrsal*, in which Goethe's words to Schopenhauer:

> Willst Du Dich Deines Wertes freuen,
> So musst der Welt Du Wert verleihen,

were quoted in connection with the new desire for a simpler and more concrete view of life. The expressionists had made the mistake of overlooking the simpler realities of existence; they had cast their eyes to

> the waste beyond God's peace,
> To maddening freedom and bewildering light,

and thereby had neglected to establish sure foundations
within the world of finite existence. The beginning of the
reaction is mirrored in Fritz von Unruh's lecture on
Goethe, *Stirb und Werde* (1922), in which the emphasis
is laid on the power of art to mould individuals into a
community. Indeed one of the most positive aspects
of the new realism lay in the attempt to build a new
community out of the ruins of the old.

One of the philosophers connected with this phase was
Albert Schweizer, whose ideas, already put forward in his
Verfall und Wiederaufbau der Kultur and his *Kultur und
Ethik*, were brought into touch with his view of Goethe
in the *Gedenkrede* of 1932. Here Schweizer demands a
new conception of humanity that is sound both for the
individual and the community. He is not concerned with
the abstractness of the expressionists, but with Goethe
proclaims a "personal" type of humanity inspired by
simple and noble intentions. Then, he says, Goethe's
hope:

> Aber es siege der Mut
> In dem gesunden Geschlecht!

will be realised.

The key to Schweizer's view of life is found in his
phrase "Ehrfurcht vor dem Leben," which might also
be described as the focus-point of the new realism. In
his essay *Dank an Goethe*[1] Hermann Hesse uses the same
phrase to define his debt to Goethe during the period of
his life which fell within the span of the movement.
The same tendency to emphasise terrestrial values is
found in Thomas Mann's essay on Goethe's *Wahlverwandtschaften* (1925).[2] Mann describes Goethe as the
child of nature, and maintains that the novel depicts "die
Macht der Natur" and "die Naturgebundenheit des
Menschen."[3]

---

[1] *Die Neue Rundschau*, April, 1932.   [2] *Ibid.*, June, 1925.

[3] For a commentary on Mann's conception of *Die Wahlverwandtschaften*, cf. the end of Max Sommerfeld's essay on this work in this *Goethe
in Umwelt und Folgezeit*, Leiden, 1935.

In no writer of the new realism does its close connection to Goethe reveal itself more distinctly or with greater poetic effect than in Hans Carossa. It would be an overwhelming task to define in one section of a lecture all that Goethe has meant to Carossa. From his autobiography *Führung und Geleit* 1933 we learn of Carossa's early admiration for Goethe, for *Faust II*, *Der Westöstliche Divan*, the *Wanderjahre* and *Die Metamorphose der Pflanzen*.

Like Goethe, Carossa has written entirely on the basis of his own experience. It is especially the later Goethe who has influenced Carossa, the Goethe who, looking back on the events of his youth, saw in them stages in a gradual development. The autobiographical *motif* of *Führung und Geleit* is thus the same as that of *Dichtung und Wahrheit*. With the later Goethe Carossa shares also the philosophical acceptance of the inevitable renunciation that is the lot of man. "Die vorbereitende Schule," he writes, "der Überwindungen ist gut," and again: "Selig, wer da überwindet." Goethe's conception of the organic development of life was a consolation to Carossa in a time of national disruption, and in *Führung und Geleit* he quotes Goethe's remark that all that is valuable is preserved in the past. Strikingly reminiscent of the ageing Goethe is Carossa's reference to his character Pater Mayer as "dem Entsagenden, der seine Triebe ins Geistige hinüberwandelt"—an idea that recurs in the lines:

> Wer einem Wink folgt im Sein,
> Vieles zu Einem erbaut,
> Stündlich prägt ihn der Stern,
> Und nach glühenden Jahren,
> Wenn wir irdisch erblinden,
> Reift eine grössre Natur.

The problem that underlies Carossa's work is, as might be expected in a man who wrote at a time when a new communal spirit was arising from the ruins of defeat, that of the inter-relationship of the individual and the community. Here he links up with Goethe's ideas, as

found in the *Metamorphose der Pflanzen*, of the relationship of plant life to the life of man. That Carossa has
studied Goethe's scientific writings is evident, not only
from his own confession, but also from his praise in
Führung und Geleit of Goethe's essay *Über den Granit*.
It is, however, to the *Geheimnisse des reifen Lebens* that
we must look to discover Carossa's most mature judgment
on the nature of plant life. Here he develops his theory
of the continuous but unconscious evolution of the plant
with its repercussion on our own spiritual life, and of the
spiritual influences that issue from the world of nature.

These observations on the evolution of nature have a
parallel in Carossa's conception of social life. The community that he envisages to take the place of that destroyed by the War resembles in principle that which
Goethe describes in *Die Wahlverwandtschaften*. It will
be drawn together, he thinks, not by external factors,
such as law or marriage, but by the spiritual ties that bind
man to man. Such a relationship is that between Gion
and Cynthia in *Der Arzt Gion*. Just as in *Die Wahlverwandtschaften* Ottilie's influence upon the circle in which
she lives does not cease with her death, so the personality
of Emerenz survives and remains active, not only in the
figure of her child, but also in the spiritual link that unites
this group. Like Goethe, Carossa conceived a form of
communal life that would not absorb the individual but
would be the sum total of individual lives. Goethe saw
the social ties that since the Middle Ages had drawn
mankind together break under the impact of the French
Revolution, and in *Die Wahlverwandtschaften* he sought
the way to a substitute. Carossa witnessed a similar
collapse of social life under the stress of forces released
by the War, and his answer to the problems that thus
arose is as characteristic of the new realism as it is
illuminating for Carossa's close kinship to Goethe.

In short, Goethe's doctrine of "Stirb und Werde"
stands close to Carossa's conviction of the fertility of
nature's processes. "Das Werdende, das ewig wirkt und

lebt" finds expression, for instance, in Emerenz, whose death is a self-sacrifice in the cause of life. Thus to Carossa, as to Goethe, death and destruction are but problems that can only be understood in the light of their positive corollary, and to express this idea Carossa borrows Goethe's conception of the "Mothers" of *Faust II*:

> Sammle Fund und Fund
> Und weihe sie dem Reich der Mütter still zurück!
> Dort mag Verlassenes neuer Form entgegenruhn.
>
> .   .   .   .
>
> Verwahren und Verhehlen kann zur Wende-Zeit
> Ein frommer Dienst sein.

The description of the doctor in the *Rumänisches Tagebuch* who feels "ein grenzenloses Vetrauen in die strömenden und untergrabenden Kräfte der Welt" is as applicable to Goethe as to Carossa. It is not merely the fact that Carossa's work is rich in direct references to Goethe's writings, such as that to Goethe's poem *Selige Sehnsucht* in Carossa's *Von Lust zu Lust*, which justifies us in seeing in Carossa Goethe's greatest contribution to any single poet of the century, with the possible exception of Hauptmann, but rather our perception that it is in Goethe that Carossa's view of life finds its magnetic centre.

Side by side with this positive element in the new realism represented by Carossa there is to be found within the movement a negative tendency, whose outlook was coloured by doubt and resignation born of the tragic events that were still fresh in the memory. In 1924 Werner Mahrholz published an essay entitled *Bemerkungen über Goethe und das Problem der Bildung*,[1] in which Goethe is depicted as the man who examined all problems of existence at their root, without however finding a solution which can help us to solve the pressing questions of to-day. In brief "Goethe der Klassiker ist uns gestorben." It is typical of the negative side of the new realism that, on the one hand, with Mahrholz, it attempted to dethrone the idealism of the classical Goethe,

---

[1] Published in *Der Rufer*.

and, on the other, exalted the domestic circumstances of his life. Thus in these years there appeared a number of novels, now fallen into oblivion, dealing with aspects of his private affairs, and which include Burg's *Alles um Liebe: Ein Goethe-Roman*, Langheinrich's *Kätchen Schönkopf*, Drygalski's *Im Schatten der Titanen* and Linzen's *Zug der Gestalten*.[1]

As we approach the literature of our own time we are faced with the emergence of the new nationalism with its critical, almost arrogant view of Goethe. In his essay *Von der zeitlichen Aufgabe des Romans und der Novelle* (1927) Hans Grimm points to the fact that Goethe wrote for a limited and cultured public, but that now literature has a wider task, a "nationale Funktion." The age of Goethe therefore "ist dem Volke etwas schuldig geblieben," and is no basis for the nationalistic conception of art. Kolbenheyer demands, in his book *Stimme* (1932), that German literature should liberate itself from those foreign influences which constitute the background of Goethe's work. Richard Benz is more compromising in his *Geist und Reich* (1933), when he claims Goethe as a forerunner of the new nationalism. His evidence includes reference to Iphigenia, who was seeking not the art but the country of the Greeks, to Goethe's words "Im Anfang war die Tat," to his alleged failure in Italy to find the un-German quality of form, and he contends that the belief that Goethe attained his highest art during his classical period is a "Bildungsmissverständnis." Perhaps the most balanced interpretation of Goethe from the standpoint of the new nationalism is to be found in Binding's *Der deutsche und der humanistische Gedanke im Angesicht der Zukunft* (1937), where the hellenism of the age of Goethe is represented as a necessary stage towards the eventual coming-of-age of the German spirit: "Wenn einmal die Gestalt des Griechenjünglings abgelöst sein wird von der deutschen Gestalt, wenn wir selber Vorbild

[1] Cf. Bock and Weitzel's catalogue of literary works *Der historische Roman als Begleiter der Weltgeschichte*, 2 vols. Leipzig, n.d.

werden, selber Inbegriff geworden sind, dann mag der griechische Jüngling vor dem deutschen in den Schatten treten; in den Schatten deutschen Wesens. Wir werden uns dessen nicht zu schämen brauchen, dass der es war, der uns dazu geholfen hat ihn zu überwinden." There is little doubt that, for the new nationalism as a whole, however, Goethe has been little more than an interesting historical factor and only to a neglible extent an inspirational force.

National-socialism has brought with it the inevitable "official" view of Goethe, but the attempt to trace any real relationship between its literature and the work of Goethe yields no positive results. It confirms the impression that the waning of his influence in the literary movements, as noticed in the new nationalism, has continued and increased in the writers of national-socialism. In three books that have appeared since 1932, in which Goethe's contribution to present-day Germany is examined,[1] there is significantly scarcely a reference to a creative writer. If it is to fulfil the mission of furthering the cause of the state, German poetry in the Third Empire can have little use for "der Dichtung Schleier aus der Hand der Wahrheit."

We have seen that the twentieth century has already witnessed the rise and fall of a bewildering sequence of literary movements, though the beginning of this procession must be sought at the close of the last century. Naturalism, neo-romanticism, impressionism, neo-classicism, expressionism, new realism, new nationalism and national-socialism have all represented to their protagonists what they have hopefully regarded as the progress of literature. None of these movements has found it possible to overlook a poet of Goethe's stature, though some may have studied him only to recast his ideas or to reject them.

---

[1] Paul Vogt, *Goethes Lebensanschauung als Erlebnis der heutigen Zeit,* Berlin, 1937; Paul Lorentz, *Goethes Spuren im geistigen Ringen der Gegenwart,* Weimar, 1933; Wilhelm Fehse, *Goethe im Lichte des neuen Werdens,* Braunschweig, 1935.

As Max Halbe has recently written,[1] Goethe lived his life upon so many spiritual planes that his appeal to posterity has been varied. To some naturalists he was an unsympathetic figure, the *ne plus ultra* of an unwelcome tradition. There were, however, followers of the movement who, as a result of their kinship with Storm and Stress, felt a brotherly affection for the young Goethe. Others proclaimed him to be the supreme poet of evolution, the model for the new age. To the neoromantics he was above all the poet of ethereal beauty, of subtle and perfect form, the mirror of the soul, the herald of world-festivity and the champion of a culture which they tried in vain to graft on to their own time. The expressionists, in spite of their similarities of style to the language of the young Goethe, disowned him, but *Faust* became, nevertheless, the fountain-head of much of their own dramatic work. The violent anti-bourgeois attitude of the expressionists was countered by the view of such writers as Thomas Mann to whom Goethe, as the representative of the "Bürgertum," was ever an inspiration and a cherished ideal. To Carossa, in whom we find the new realist conception of Goethe, it was the old Goethe who appealed, with his care of tradition and his knowledge of the fertility of existence. The decline of Goethe's rôle in the literary movements of the century begins with the new nationalism and becomes unmistakable in the works of national-socialist writers.

Nevertheless, the spirit of Goethe lives on in German literature. Hauptmann[2] is still writing, and a recent

[1] In his autobiography *Jahrhundertwende*, Danzig, 1935, p. 11.

[2] Hauptmann's debt to Goethe does not fall within the scope of this paper since his approach has been personal and only to a very limited extent the expression of a movement or movements. It is just touched upon in the essay "Goethe and present-day German writers" in the *Goethe Centenary Papers*, edited by Martin Schütze, Chicago and London, 1933. For a similar reason Rilke's relationship to Goethe's thought has been omitted; it is dealt with fully by Eva Seidels (*Rilkes Wendung zu Goethe*) and Eberhard Kretschmar (*Goethe und Rilke*) in the *Vierteljahrschrift der Goethe-Gesellschaft*, 1937, in Kretschmar's book on *Goethe und Rilke*, Dresden, 1937, and in Lisa de Boor's brief essay "Rainer Maria Rilkes Weg zu Goethe" in the *Goetheanum*, 9 June, 1935.

lecture of Carossa testifies to his unshaken faith in Goethe. Outside Germany, in the literature of the *émigrés*, Goethe's *humanitas* is still a seminal force, and Thomas Mann's periodical *Mass und Wert*[1] calls Goethe to bear witness to the justice of its cause. Within Germany the exhilarating hellenism of young poets, such as Weinheber and Jünger, suggests the possibility that the whirligig of time may yet bring in his revenges and vindicate the claim that, from the beginning of the twentieth century till to-day, there are few aspects of the successive literary movements that cannot be summarised in terms of their conception of Goethe.

[1] Cf. the Preface to the first number. Extracts have appeared from Mann's *Lotte in Weimar* dealing with Charlotte Buff's later visit to Goethe.

Chapter II

GERMAN EXPRESSIONISM AND THE CONTEMPORARY ENGLISH STAGE

Below the tomato blobs was a band of white with vertical black stripes, to which he could assign no meaning whatever, till someone else came by, murmuring: "What expression he gets with his foreground!" Expression? Of what? Soames went back to his seat. The thing was "rich," as his father would have said, and he wouldn't give a damn for it. Expression! Ah! they were all Expressionists now, he had heard, on the Continent. So it was coming here too, was it? He remembered the first wave of influenza in 1887—or—8—hatched in China, so they said. He wondered where this—this Expressionism—had been hatched. The thing was a regular disease!

JOHN GALSWORTHY, *The Forsyte Saga.*

EXPRESSIONISM came to the forefront in Germany in the years immediately before the outbreak of the War of 1914–18. It was not by chance that this was so; for, by its very nature, expressionism, with its cult of the surprising, the unexpected and the grotesque, was the mirror of an age of changing values. This branch of European modernism thrived on the atmosphere which surrounded German life and letters from about 1910 onwards. New vistas were being opened up in the world of science and discovery, and in the sphere of culture the old standards were being dethroned with complete disrespect of persons. It is true that neo-romanticism, even at the time of the outbreak of the War, was still trying to preserve the ideas and beauties for which man craves in his moments of introspection and imagination. But the reign of neo-romanticism was for all intents and purposes over. Life was threatened by the stern actualities of the machine age. Wars and rumours of wars disturbed the noon-tide peace of neo-romantic literature. Reinhard Johannes Sorge is typical of the new expressionist generation when in his play

Der Bettler (written in 1911) he turns against some of the neo-romantics, such as Hardt and Vollmoeller, and demands that the course of literature shall be directed by poets whose yearnings centre not on the legendary past but upon a new and better future. Thus with the expressionist generation literature becomes more than the companion of idle hours; it is transformed, in a manner akin to the poetry of Stefan George, into an instrument of social change and improvement. Like naturalism, it seeks out the horrible aspects of human existence and does not flinch from depicting the darkest vice and crime of mankind. No corner of life amid the squalor of large towns could exceed in its ugliness the horrors sometimes painted by the writers of Expressionism. Rilke's descriptions in the *Aufzeichnungen des Malte Laurids Brigge* (1910) and before that in the latter sections of *Das Stundenbuch* (1898–1903) had pointed the way to a recognition that life had many more sides than the average neo-romantic poet realised. Naturalism, however, though it was fascinated, as if by a morbid curiosity, by the evils of a time that seemed so decidedly out of joint, could point to no concrete remedy. The "Freie Bühne" therefore resembled the dissecting room rather than the operating theatre. Even Rilke, the intrinsic value of whose poetic output, of course, surpasses that of any of the actual expressionists, in this particular respect was only a passive describer. His familiarity with Paris had opened his eyes but had not revealed the Promised Land.

Expressionism therefore was a literary movement with a social programme. Even at the very outset of the movement poets like Heym and Trakl (both destined to die an early death) were preoccupied with describing, with a reforming zeal, the social and economic evils of their time and its present discontents. Think for instance of Heym's poem "Hunger" or the theme of "Die Vorstadt." Stadler too, in many of the poems in the collection *Der Aufbruch* (1914), was portraying the horrors of the

world, in which his lot was cast, in terms calculated to
whip indignation into practical measures of reform.
With the outbreak of the War the tone of expressionism changed. Its temper was quickened, its tone
became more violent and its purpose more threatening.
The underlying theme of the War poetry of Werfel
("Der Krieg"), of the contributors to René Schickele's
Die Weissen Blätter, which were issued from Switzerland
whither he and a number of like-minded friends had
taken refuge, of Unruh (whose drama *Ein Geschlecht*
(1916) will surely take its place among the significant
plays of modern German literature) and of Toller (whose
reforming zeal too often outstripped his poetic sensitive-
ness)—the *leitmotif* of poetry such as this was *J'accuse*.
With the rise of expressionism to the cultural leadership
of Germany, German literature became the vehicle of
political controversy, the weapon of an idealistic and angry
generation, and the passionate revealer of man's in-
humanity to man.

As the War dragged on and the fate of humankind
became more and more precarious, expressionism
developed in scope and few writers were able to avoid
altogether its challenging influence. Even Rilke, as a
glance at the *Duineser Elegien* will show, felt the impact
of its aesthetic principles. In 1917 the periodical *Die
Aktion*, founded a few years earlier, attached to itself the
sub-title "Organ of the most radical friends of peace for
anti-national politics and culture" and thereby reflected
the rampant indignation which, with growing vehemence,
was invading the minds of Germans, especially of the
younger generation. Hasenclever sums up the intentions of his fellow poets in the poem *1917*:

> Halte wach den Hass.   Halte wach das Leid.
> Brenne weiter, Flamme!   Es naht die Zeit!

The poet had become the demagogue, fearless in his
purpose and desperately unscrupulous in his methods:

> Der Dichter meidet strahlende Akkorde,
> Er stösst durch Tuben, peitscht die Trommel schrill.
> Er reisst das Volk auf mit gehackten Sätzen.

There was a double reason for this increased violence of tone. In the first place, the Russian Revolution of 1917 had suggested that the pacifist and ultra-democratic ideals of the expressionists were finding practical realisation elsewhere in the world, and that the New World which the expressionists sought to proclaim was in the process of being born. Secondly, the change can be explained by the internal situation of Germany. The War, recognised by German public opinion in its early stages as a war of defence, was in its eyes now altering in its intentions. The rise of Ludendorff to the position of virtual dictator in 1916 and the foundation of the Fatherland Party, set on large-scale annexations in the event of victory, unmasked the political leaders of Germany in the eyes of the expressionists. Between the humanitarian ideals of a New Community, based upon international co-operation in a world without victors and vanquished, and the military programme of those responsible for Germany's fortunes, a great gulf, it seemed, was fixed.

The development of the situation on the military front encouraged, however, the expressionists. The prospect of a military victory receded, as time went on, and it became clear that Germany's defeat was imminent. The story of the last months of the War is too well known to need repetition. The mutiny in the German Fleet was the beginning of the actual collapse of the German Empire, and on 9th November, 1918, Imperial Germany was "ashes under Unicorn."

The reactions of the expressionists were immediate and unambiguous. The fall of the Hohenzollern régime was in expressionist circles greeted rapturously as the close of the spiritual tyranny of mankind. René Schickele felt on that day that he was "tangibly in Heaven." Mankind, so the expressionists believed, had learnt its lesson and had struck its tents, ready to begin the "march into the modern age after the burden of the Middle Ages had been thrown aside."

With the removal of the censorship the scope of expressionism was at once widened. The anthologies which had before their suppression served as the vehicle of expressionist ideals were now freed from the censor and blossomed out again in their former enthusiasm. Their titles give some idea of their tone: "Comrades of Mankind," "Poems in support of World Revolution" and "The Dawn of Mankind." Rosa Luxemburg, the socialist leader, was celebrated by Becher with an almost ludicrous enthusiasm:

> O Würze paradiesischer Auen :
> Du Einzige! Du Heilige! O Weib.

By this time, out of the political ideals of the expressionists there had crystallised a special group of writers, within the movement itself, who termed themselves "activists." Their interests were almost exclusively centred on political programmes. They were in the first place preachers, and only poets in so far as poetry was a means of propaganda. Their views were predominantly revolutionary and communistic. The collapse of the German Empire acted as a special stimulus to this section of the movement which naturally welcomed with great enthusiasm the foundation, albeit for a brief spell only, of a Soviet republic in Munich in 1919 in which Ernst Toller played a leading part.

This survey of expressionism must be brief and can only touch on certain aspects of the movement which are of importance for the second section of the subject under review. But before this stage is reached it is important to recount, again in outline only, the story of the decline and fall of expressionism. It is soon told, though it is not the least interesting chapter in its history.

The origins of expressionism are to be found in the general spiritual unrest which marked the cultural affairs of pre-War Germany. From the time of the German victory in the war against France in 1870–1 to the beginning of the Great War, Germany passed through a time characterised by the absence of any settled spiritual or social values. The rapid development of industry and capitalism and the rapidly expanding political power of the country, together with the several important political crises which characterised those years, left Germany unstable and insecure. The rise of a generation of writers who were profoundly dissatisfied with the social position of the individual and with the social effectiveness and ideals of the state added to this feeling of unrest. The result was that the years just before the outbreak of the War were a time of deep unrest. Ideas and ideals were in the melting pot. It was a time of transition between two worlds, one weary of the past and the other, as yet, powerless to be born.

It was on such soil that the flower of expressionism took seed and on such soil only could it flourish. It was in a very real sense the literature of youth, the mouthpiece of adolescent longings and dissatisfaction. Indeed one leading expressionist accounted for his discontinued interest in its ideals by pointing to the fact that he and his fellows had reached maturity. I quote from Hasenclever:

> Wir haben den Sturm der Freiheit geläutet.
> Wir waren Jünglinge. Jetzt sind wir Mann. . . .
> Ach, die Taten des dröhnenden Mundes
> Sind vergangen. Tritt ein in die Reih!

The situation in Germany after the War was for only a short time favourable to a continuance of expressionism. The Treaty of Versailles seemed to those who, within the framework of the movement, had proclaimed the all-embracing humanitarian ideals of the New Community peopled by the New Man, to be the death-blow of such far-flung yearnings. Germany lay prostrate beneath the control of the Allies, and, although the expressionists wept few tears over the passing of Hohenzollern Germany, they wept bitterly for the rape of her spiritual self-respect and for the removal of any foundations upon which the New World could be built. For the New Man, they felt, who was to have rejoiced in justice and to have preached the "everlasting gospel," would cut a poor and miserable figure in a world conditioned by the terms of Versailles.

And so it was that in the years that immediately followed the end of the War, we find little trace of the pristine buoyancy of early expressionism. The movement, it is true, lived on, but its wings were clipped, and its hopes were finally shattered by the occupation of the Ruhr in 1923. At this point a new factor began to operate against any further existence of the movement. It was said above that its point of departure had been a time of spiritual unrest. Now, from about 1924, a new note of confidence began to creep into Germany's spiritual life. The policy of agreement, marked by the Treaty of Locarno in 1925 and the entry of Germany into the League of Nations the following year, robbed expressionism of what had so encouraged it in its early years. In place of expressionism we find the objective restraint of the new realism, which is characteristic of this return to stability.

We now come to a discussion of the expressionist drama, for it is this aspect of the movement that has exercised the greatest influence on literature outside Germany and which has left its mark quite definitely on the contemporary English theatre.

The nature of the expressionist drama is derived naturally from the expressionist view of life. The expressionist is essentially a visionary; he is not concerned with finite reality as such but he is only interested in it so far as he sees it as the mirror of God, the symbol of eternity. This point of view forms the central theme of Edschmid's pamphlet *Über den Expressionismus in der Literatur* (1919). He sees life as a constant yearning and progress towards the infinite which he attempts to attain through vision and ecstacy. Throughout expressionism therefore there is found an acute recognition of the conflicting claims of the finite and the infinite, a problem which is most profoundly formulated by Franz Kafka, whose novels all turn on this question. The expressionist pursues, as it were, the infinite; he wrestles with it, determined to grasp it and to understand it, and he values his own life and work only so far as they are successful in this search. On the other hand, he recognises (though he seldom says so explicitly) that, as Werfel remarked in one of his plays, "all eternity flees from fulfilment." Here is a dualism which renders the expressionist programme ultimately incapable of any concrete realisation and which as much as any external circumstance contributed to its close.

Accordingly one branch of the expressionist drama is concerned above all with interpreting to man his rôle on earth and in directing him to a faith in his infinite and eternal calling. This branch, concerned as it is with the inter-relationship of two worlds, resorts frequently to a parallel series of actions, one representing the events within the finite sphere and the other portraying an action within the greater world of infinite reality. Such a play is Kornfeld's *Himmel und Hölle* (1919). The theme of this work is the process of recognition, which the characters experience, that true existence consists in putting off the shackles of an earthbound, erroneous reality and in striking new roots, as it were, in the world which they gradually come to recognise in its true nature. It may be noted that these plays often reveal an unmistakeable influence of *Faust II*. The close of Kornfeld's play will indicate this:

Keine Seele ist verloren,
Jeder Mensch ist auserwählt,
Jeder Mensch ist auserkoren
Trotz Teufeln und Dämonen,
Dass er dem Göttlichen sich vermählt!
So schweben wir, schweben wir, schweben wir auf,
Unsterbliche Seelen, unsterblich in Äonen.

The theme of this work is found in different form in Ernst Barlach's *Der Arme Vetter* (1918). The story centres round a group of people waiting for a boat on which they are to travel. As they wait, they chat about "ghosts," by which are meant the people and events which had constituted the action of the play. Two characters, the Poor Cousin and Fräulein Isenbarn, found their "true high calling." The conclusion at which Barlach hints through this veil of unreality is that the world of finite existence is but a place of "ghosts." In it nothing is real. Only those who, like the two people in question, have found their "calling" recognise the true world, the world of infinite reality.

To those familiar with Barlach's play, T. S. Eliot's new play, *The Family Reunion*, must appear less strange and unexpected than to those who do not approach it *via* their knowledge of German expressionism. It is one of a number of recent plays that show that the English stage is at present experiencing a wave that resembles very strikingly German expressionism. Of course, past instances indicate that some time always elapses between a continental literary phase and its actual reception in England, and this custom seems to be observed in the case of expressionism.

Let us examine briefly *The Family Reunion*. The play is based on the story of Orestes. It is the story of one pursued by the Furies. Like Eugene O'Neill in his *Mourning Becomes Electra*, Eliot has transformed this legend into something rich and very strange and made it into a problem of life in our own time. The setting of the play is accordingly realistic. A family is assembled to celebrate the Mother's seventieth birthday and is awaiting the arrival of Harry, her eldest son. The company consists also of two of Harry's uncles and two of his aunts. These four persons constitute themselves at various points of the action into a chorus and comment, in a manner familiar to everyone who knows some German expressionist plays, on the workings of fate and the other world upon this finite world. There is also Agatha, the Mother's sister, who of all the characters stands closest to the drama of expressionism. Her part is identical with

that of Fräulein Isenbarn in Barlach's *Der Arme Vetter*.
She is a figure whose part, measured in lines spoken, is
small and yet philosophically she is perhaps the most
significant member of the cast. Like Fräulein Isenbarn
and the Poor Cousin, she has discovered her "true,
high meaning." She has recognised the shackles of
finite existence and, through this recognition, is enabled
to live according to the demands of the higher reality,
which she sees as in a glass darkly. The hero is Harry,
and he passes through exactly the same experience as the
Poor Cousin in Barlach's play. He experiences, like so
many characters in expressionist plays, through a
"transformation" (*Wandlung*). He was once responsible
for the death of his wife and this remembrance weighs
upon him and pursues him, as the Furies pursued
Orestes. Through Agatha, however, he learns of the true
nature of life and of the true task awaiting man. He
thereby liberates himself from the pursuing phantoms and,
realising that all is vanity but man's higher self, he
announces that he will follow the "bright angels":

> It is love and terror
> Of what waits and wants me, and will not let me fall.
> I must follow the bright angels.

Here we find that same idea that man must be changed
through contact with the infinite, with that higher life
that awaits him, and that the life of man, judged from
any but this viewpoint, is as nothing. It is not only in
its theme that this play looks back to expressionism. Its
setting, too, recalls it. The all-pervading presence of the
pursuing spirits imparts just that element of the super-
real without which expressionist drama is impossible.
Throughout the play the two conflicting worlds stand side
by side until at the close the one is rendered vain and
purposeless by the admitted claims and realities of the
other. And the chorus of uncles and aunts adds just
the same degree of the grotesque as is found in the
prototypes of Eliot's play in Germany.

If *The Family Reunion* is reminiscent of Barlach, it is

of such writers as Becker and Weismantel that we think
in connection with Mr. Priestley's play, *Johnson over
Jordan*. This play, like so many expressionist plays,
is what can be termed a "Stationendrama." That is to
say, it depicts the hero at various stages of his existence
both in this world and in the world of infinity, and depicts
a gradual progression towards his ultimate attainment of
the life beyond the grave. This branch of the expressionist drama came from the medieval mystery play which
had been revived by Vollmoeller (*Das Mirakel*, 1912).
Priestley designates his play as a "Modern Morality"
and as such it belongs to the same lineage as Weismantel's
Totentanz 1921, and Becker's *Das Letzte Gericht*.
Priestley takes over more of the expressionist stage-
technique even than Eliot. Throughout the play we
find all the elements of the expressionist drama, from
the frequent incursion of the grotesque, the use of the
chorus, and the super-real, to the division of the action
and setting into two separate halves; each act consists of
two scenes, the first playing within this world while the
second always is concerned with the fate of Johnson's
soul after his death. It is not the least characteristic
feature of the play, from our present point of view, that
the whole thing ends with a grandiose vision of a future
that transcends all that man can experience on earth.

Both these plays end on a positive note. Like all
expressionist plays they lead the hero to a state higher
than that from which he began. We must now turn to
a group of plays which are linked to expressionism not
only by their characters and their settings but also in
that they put forward the idea of a new kingdom on
earth. Adopting sometimes the forceful rhetoric of
Hasenclever in his *Antigone* or the restrained poetry of
Unruh's *Ein Geschlecht* or *Vor der Entscheidung*, or the
visionary ecstacy of Arnold Zweig's *Jeremias*, the
expressionist is constantly concerned with putting forward his idea of a new world in which men will be ruled
by love. Such a view of life demands a new conception

of man, who must abandon his traditional slogans and his familiar ways. He must put on the New Man; he must re-orientate himself and his life and he must above all sacrifice his happiness and comforts in the interests of humanity, which is seeking a leader towards this high goal. It is curious that expressionism, in its origins and in so many of its tenets profoundly democratic, should adopt in its ethics a standpoint that in one respect is fundamentally opposed to a democratic "Weltanschauung." For again and again the expressionist sets up on a pedestal the man whose virtue is that he surpasses his fellow-men and is a leader amongst wandering sheep. There is surely something here of the legacy of the Nietzschean Superman.

Leadership and sacrifice seen against the background of a bleeding and distressed humanity is indeed the basic experience that informs almost all expressionist poetry. This is frequently a summons away from the empty conventions and surface delights of an over-civilised world back to the essential elements from which life itself proceeded and to which it must be once more guided. The poetry, for instance, of Stephen Spender is rich in its treatment of this theme. His "goal" is summed up in his words:

> Man shall be man,

and, to prepare the way for this great state of man, he calls to men to cease dalliance with the empty and unworldly forms of beauty:

> Leave your gardens, your singing feasts,
> Your dreams of suns circling before our sun,
> Of heaven after our world . . .,

and he cries to them to bring about the new age ruled by

> The palpable and obvious love of man for man,

which will supersede the "failure of cathedrals" and "the declared insanity of our rulers." "Haunted" by the "emptiness" of the civilised life around him, Spender proclaims the glory of those who have sacrificed themselves in the cause of the new world to which he looks forward:

> The names of those who in their lives have fought for life
> Who wore at their hearts the fire's centre.
> Born of the sun they travelled a short while towards the sun,
> And left the vivid air signed with their honour.

Within the last four years three plays have appeared by Messrs. Auden and Isherwood which give dramatic form to ideals similar to those of Spender and which reveal further evidence that the influence of expressionism is alive in this country. For *The Dog beneath the Skin*, *The Ascent of F6*, and *On the Frontier* not only borrow all the external paraphernalia of German expressionism (witness the well-worn device of the alternating sequence of realistic and super-real scenes and the recurring use of the chorus), but take over lock, stock and barrel its ethical programme. The epilogue of *The Dog beneath the Skin* may be quoted as a summary of the spiritual cravings and the ethical demands of the movement:

Semi-Chorus II

Mourn not for these; these are ghosts who chose their pain,
Mourn rather for yourselves; and your inability to make up your minds
Whose hours of self-hatred and contempt were all your majesty and crisis,
Choose therefore that you may recover: both your charity and your place
Determining not this that we have lately witnessed: but another country
Where grace may grow outward and be given praise
Beauty and virtue be vivid there.

Semi-Chorus I

> Where time flows on as chalk stream clear
> And lovers by themselves forgiven
> The whole dream genuine, the charm mature
> Walk in the great and general light
> In their delight a part of heaven
> Its furniture and choir.

Chorus

> To each his need: from each his power.

Here we find not only the expressionist idea of the unreality of the temporal forms of life and the conception of the splendid stature to which man will attain in a world which knows not the cramping restrictions of time and space, but also the expressionist faith in the ultimate fulfilment of man's purpose, beauty and virtue. Space makes impossible any adequate treatment of these intriguing plays, but the reader should bear in mind, as he follows Ransom (in *The Ascent of F6*) and Eric (in *On the Frontier*) to their symbolic deaths, the expressionist proclamation of the coming reign of love, to which each individual self-sacrifice is regarded as a stepping-stone. (Is there not an obvious link between these English plays and those many expressionist "visions" which figured so frequently on the German theatre during the reign of the movement—between, for instance, the visionary motive of Ransom's and Eric's deaths and Tiona Betty's vision in Alfred Brust's drama *Der Ewige Mensch?*)

> They die to make men just
> And worthy of the earth.

Expressionism in Germany and its counterpart in this country do not coincide in every detail, even if one overlooks the time-lapse, but not even the most superficial observer can fail to be struck by similarity of purpose, which is to proclaim loud and long and with all the resources of poetry and the stage the glory of man's rôle and his ultimate restoration to freedom and honour— and it so happens that English dramatists have adopted precisely the same ways and means.

One play remains to be considered, Spender's *Trial of a Judge*. Mr. Spender having admitted with regards to expressionism, that he has had "a certain experience of it," one is not surprised to find that his play is deeply indebted to the tradition established by the German expressionists. Reference was made above to the activist branch of the movement, to those poets who were concerned exclusively with setting up a political programme. It is to this branch of the movement that Mr. Spender is most akin, though it must be stated that his poetical powers far exceed those of most of his activist forbears in

Germany. In theme and method there is no great difference between his play and Hasenclever's *Antigone*. In both the theme is the pursuit of a new political gospel which will ensure that the spirit of man shall be free. In the character of the Judge we find the typical expressionist motif of spiritual "transformation" and in Hummeldorf and the Judge's wife we have the inevitable use of the grotesque, while throughout the play run the alternating real and super-real scenes. It is noteworthy that just as in Germany it was the expressionist rather than the activists who were truly successful in handling the grotesque elements, so Mr. Spender's powers in this direction must be rated as inferior to those of Messrs. Auden and Isherwood as revealed in *The Dog beneath the Skin*. Like the activists, Mr. Spender seems to have been determined that his play should be as up-to-date as the age in which it was written, and behind all the outward happenings (ranging from fiction to an episode claiming to have been enacted in a Nazi concentration camp) lurks the growing problem of Fascism. Thus in *Trial of a Judge* the technical means and devices of the German drama of twenty or thirty years ago are brought to bear upon a problem that has now passed from the sheltered sphere of political speculation into the burning arena of war.

The whirligig of time does indeed bring in his revenges. Expressionism, reported missing in Germany nearly twenty years ago (though the careful observer can find its traces in German thought since its actual *démise*) has turned up hale and hearty on the contemporary English stage.[1]

[1] It should be pointed out that Eliot's *Murder in the Cathedral* represents an example of the historical expressionist drama. It has not been discussed in this survey owing to lack of space. A characterisation of some German forerunners of this branch of the movement will be found in *Expressionism in German Life, Literature and the Theatre* (1910–1924), by Richard Samuel and R. Hinton Thomas, Cambridge, 1939, p. 63 ff.

CHAPTER III

NOTES ON SOME UNPUBLISHED PAPERS OF R. J. SORGE

A CONTRIBUTION RELATING TO THE GENESIS OF GERMAN EXPRESSIONISM

SUFFICIENT work has now been done on the early expressionist writers in Germany to make clear the general nature of this movement at the time when it first began to make itself felt as a potent force in the spiritual life of the nation. We have therefore a fairly true picture of the contribution to expressionism of such writers as Heym, Stadler and Trakl, in whose work some tendencies in German literature from about 1910 are reflected. As yet, however, little research has been carried out on what may be called the prenatal period of expressionism.[1]

Reinhard Johannes Sorge is remembered chiefly because of his play *Der Bettler*, which, first conceived[2] in September 1911, was completed in January 1912. Not only does Sorge reveal himself in *Der Bettler* as the poet "der zweifellos als der erste in Deutschland die Form ertastet hat, die man später 'expressionistisch' taufen sollte,"[3] but also as the first bearer of expressionist ideas and ideals in general. There is much of Sorge still unpublished which throws light on the embryonic

---

[1] Cf., however, Ferd. Jos. Scheider, *Victor Hadwiger* (1878–1911). *Ein Beitrag zur Geschichte des Expressionismus in der deutschen Dichtung der Gegenwart*, Halle, 1921.

[2] Cf. *Unser Weg* by Susanne M. Sorge, Münich, 1924, p. 13.

[3] Julius Bab, *Richard Dehmel*, Leipzig, 1926, p. 311.

development of the expressionist ideal in the years before *Der Bettler*.[1] Except in a few isolated cases nothing has been published that Sorge wrote previous to 1910. The works written between 1910 and *Der Bettler* have been made public[2] and also those belonging to his later years.

The MSS. indicate that Sorge began imaginative writing in earnest in 1908 when he was seventeen years old. Before this year there are only some poems in the traditional style. To 1908 belongs however, *Kinder der Erde; eine episch-dramatische Dichtung*, which represents one of Sorge's first steps along the road that was to lead to *Der Bettler*. Much is mere imitation. There are unmistakable echoes of *Faust I*, and Sorge adopts, though inconsistently, the spelling used by George.[3] This work consists of four parts: Frühling, Sommer, Herbst and Winter, and of conversations mainly between Der Alte and Der Jüngere. The former is seeking an answer to the "welträtsel" and he finds it, on the advice of his younger friend, by surrendering himself to the wider experience of life. In the words of Der Jüngere to him in this connection we find significant stress upon "Geist," which plays such a large part in expressionism proper:

> Da lösen sich des geistes irdsche Fesseln
> Die Seele schweift hinaus ins weite all,
> Durchfliegt so schnell die hohen sonnenräume,
> Des göttlichen lichtes unendlichen schwall
> Verwirklicht werden alle deine Träume,
> Und alles wissen scheint dir hohler schall
> Du schwebst gleich einem Gotte in den höhen
> Das hohe und das tiefe kannst du sehen.

---

[1] For permission to examine and make use of works to be found in the Nachlass, I am indebted to the great kindness of Frau S. M. Sorge, the poet's widow.

[2] *Der Jüngling. Die frühen Dichtungen*, edited by Frau S. M. Sorge, München, 1925.

[3] This seems to suggest that there has been some error made in the attempt to trace Sorge's first acquaintance with the work of George. Frau Sorge (in *Unser Weg*) associates it with 1911 and Martin Rockenbach (*Reinhard Johannes Sorge*, Leipzig, o.J.) attributes it to 1910.

The play closes with a eulogy of "Geist" in a passage which to-day may be regarded as prophetic:

O wie mein geist in heisser Sehnsucht brennt
Die Tore aufzureissen und voll Mut
Mich froh zu wagen in die Geistesflut
Vom Geist getragen auf und ab zu wallen
Indessen Geistesstimmen mich umschallen
Ein ewig Meer das nimmermehr versiegt.

Further we find in this early work Sorge awakening to the desire to struggle with the mystery of life:

So dehnt sich vor mir denn ein weites Feld
Dass ich durchforschen muss ohn Rast und Ruh
Das grosse tiefe Rätsel dieser Welt,
Bis mir der Tod einst drückt die Augen zu.

This emerging earnestness in the face of life, this search for direction and for the nature and aim of existence, which were to culminate in *Der Bettler*, described by him as a "Sendung," find striking expression when he says of one of his works:[1]

Und ist auch dieses Buch ein zages Tasten
Und suchen nach dem Weg, den mir ein ehern
Gesetz in meiner Brust befiehlt zu wandern
Mein Leben lang.[2]

It is clear that in these very early documents Sorge is trying to wrestle with the problem of existence; he is seeking to define his own position and duties. In *Der Bettler* he says: "einer muss wieder für uns alle nach-sinnen"; the mission of the poet, thus defined, begins to emerge in these passages. Just as a line leads from *Der Bettler* to full expressionism, so too it may be said to go back to these fragments of 1908. The expressionist ideal is beginning to assert itself. Sorge in the same year evolved ideas which come nearer still to expressionism. He sums up two prevailing conceptions of existence.[3] One he defines as "die Auffassung der ziemlich ego-

[1] *So etwas wie Philosophie*, Heft 1, 1908, MS.
[2] Added later, October 1909.
[3] *Warum leben wir?* 1908, MS.

istischen Sich-Selbst-Vervollkommnung in der Annahme
eines späteren egoistischen Weiterwirkens." The other
is the "Auffassung der selbstlosen Hingabe an alle, zur
Lösung des Problems, selbst mit Gefahr einer Nicht-
Auferstehung." He believes that the true view is the
second, and he adds: "Diese Auffassung verlangt
ausserdem noch etwas grosses vom einzelnen: den
vollkommenen Opfermut." This conception stands very
close to Sorge's view of the mission of the poet as "die
grosse Weltgüte" (in *Der Bettler*) and leads over to the
expressionist "Opfergedanke" which is one of the
corner-stones of the movement.

The year 1908 was one of tremendous poetic activity
for Sorge.[1] In this year, one can say, he awoke to ideas
and emotions which must be regarded as prenatal stages
of expressionism. It is, therefore, a year of great importance for German literature. We can take leave of
his work during this year by quoting a fragment which
is of superlative importance for the history of expressionism. The whole of the expressionist conception of
"Geist" and all that this factor meant for German
literature from about 1912 to the end of expressionism
about 1925 is summed up in this wonderful passage:

> Manchmal ist mir so stark, so jauchzend froh ums Herz, unter den
> Klängen einer jubelnden Musik scheine ich dahinzuschiessen auf kleinem
> Nachen durch schäumende Fluten des Geistes und es ist mir, als tauche er
> oft unten in ein Wellental und versinke er im Sprühen des Geistes, dann
> aber als schwinge er sich auf und als türme er über Schaumwellen dem
> Lichte entgegen.[2]

1909 and 1910 brought for Sorge new and far-reaching
experiences, as for example the "Johannes-Erlebnis."[3]

---

[1] Besides the works already mentioned cf. MSS. *Namenloses Drama,
Novellistische Versuche, Die Alte Eiche* (drama), etc.

[2] Written at the end of the booklet containing the *Namenloses Drama*.
It therefore belongs probably to 1908.

[3] This experience cannot be dealt with here in full, but it has an importance similar to the " Maximin-Erlebnis " for George and it finds
poetical expression in the unpublished Märchen *Vom Schmetterling und
seiner Wunderblume*. Also cf. *Unser Weg*, pp. 22 ff.

Sorge continues in the *Gedanken über verschiedene Dinge* MS. his ideological searches. These were written under the influence of Nietzsche, as is indicated by such sentences as: "Schwächere Geister werden nirgend lange verweilen, sie haben nicht die Kraft, beharrlich in die Tiefen zu dringen," and: "Gebieterisch ist alles Leben," etc. He widens his dramatic field,[1] and for the first time he defines for himself his position regarding his treatment of a given theme.[2] He concludes that he must approach any subject along entirely subjective lines. The importance of this view for expressionism is seen not only in Sorge's later rejection of the treatment by Hardt and Vollmoeller of legendary subjects[3] but also in the whole approach of the later expressionists to the subject.[4] The 1908 fragments, we saw, represented the first steps in the awakening of a new and wider type of experience than that prevalent in German literature in these years; in 1909–10 he becomes conscious of the need definitely to break with the past and tradition. The world of expressionism is obviously fast approaching.

The poems, seven in all, which bear the title *Eines Narren Narrenlieder*,[5] and belong likewise to 1910, reveal new tones in German poetry and anticipate much of the expressionist poetry proper. In them we find the rhapsodic form entering poetry, uncontrolled, incoherent exclamations invade and interrupt the rhythm, and, above all, the new cosmic experience which underlies almost the whole of expressionist view of life comes to

[1] Cf. the *Indisches Drama* of which only the plan exists with its (for expressionism) so significant and prophetic figure, "die verhüllte Gestalt."

[2] In the Nachwort to his *Ergänzung des Lessing'schen Fragments "Spartakus,"* March 1910.

[3] Cf. the "Kritiker" scene in *Der Bettler* and the poem "Zukunft" (in *Der Jüngling*, pp. 152–3).

[4] Cf. for example, the subjective approach of the expressionists to antiquity (e.g. Hasenclever, *Antigone*, Werfel, *Die Troerinnen*).

[5] The madness motif was much used by Sorge as by expressionism in general. Cf. the Father (in *Der Bettler*) and the play *Die Narren*, MS.

the fore.[1] All these features are found in "Des Narren Sturmlied":

Nun hört des Narren Lied,
Des Narren Lied in der Nacht,
In der Nacht, in der Nacht
Bei Sturm und Wolkenflug......!
............Holloho.........Holloho.........
Da werf' ich ab mein Gewand,
Mein rotes Narrengewand
Jauchzend wild im Sturm......
Und schwing ein Schwert in Händen,
Ein glitzend-gleissend Schwert............
............Holloho.........Holloho.........
Hoch in die Mitternacht
Schwing ich mein glitzend Schwert......
....
Und führ' ein Ross am Zaum,
Ein wildes wiehernd Ross
............Halloho.........Halloho.........
Hoch in die Mitternacht
Bäumt sich mein witternd Ross
        .... Halloho.........
Der Welt—hei—der Welt
Der sinnlos ekeln Welt
Jauchz' ich da Ade:
Über Wolken und Wind,
Über Weiten und All
Trägt im Sturm mich mein Ross.........
............Halloh.............Halloho.........
Hin zu den Tiefen,
den dunklen Tiefen
Wo die Seelen sich einen,
Ewig sich einen in
Ewiger Heiligkeit......
....................Halloheiho.........

So klang des Narren Lied,
Des Narren Lied in der Nacht,
In der Nacht, in der Nacht
Bei Sturm und Wolkenflug.

[1] The titles of these poems are: (1) Wie der Narr an Anfang singt. (2) Des Narren Lied vom guten Bruder Tod. (3) Des Narren Nachtlied. (4) Des Narren Trinklied. (5) Des Narren Sturmlied. (6) Des Narren Traumlied. (7) Des Narren Sterbelied. Of these all are MS. except No. 2, which was published in *Orplid*, 11 Jahrg., Heft 12. Hardt's *Tantris der Narr* was probably the underlying influence.

The year 1910 saw in Sorge the real breakthrough of this cosmic "Weltanschauung." In the same year, in July, we find in another poem[1] this cosmic element recurring but with the significant addition that man figures more prominently in the centre of it. Here we find the cosmos represented as in wild movement around an individual. This baroque-expressionist feature makes the poem, which has the title "Das Drama," one of great importance as a foretaste of the direction in which German poetry was to move in a few years' time:

> Nackt wie nackte Welle
> Schau ich einen Menschen
> Am Meerufer liegen.
> Ihm zur Linken
> Starr aus Felsen
> Steilt eine Wand—
> Ihm zur Rechten
> Winddurchsungen dunkeln hochgereckte
> Stumme Cypressen—
> In die Stille
> In die Meeresstille tönt mein Machtwort
> Tönt mein mahnend Machtwort:
>
> *Mensch zum Menschen*
>
> .   .   .   .   .   .
>
> Es bebt der Mensch empor
> Der wellennackte
> Lebensmächtig dringt aus tiefsten Quellen
> Was verhalten hallend in ihm schlief:
> Quillen Qualen, funkeln Ahneshellen
> Und aus Rosenschalen fluten Wellen
> Heller Freuden, die so trunken tief
> Leuchten lässt und schwellen
> Heissversteckte Gier alldies durchbebend
> Denn ich rief mein belebend
> Mahnend Machtwort:
>
> *Mensch zum Menschen*
>
> .   .   .   .   .   .
>
> Es reckt sich meine Hand
> Die schöpferisch gedehnte
> Was aus Gründen wuchs

[1] MS.

Gründend forme ich
In lohenden Gesichten
Zu lohenden Gesichtern
Zu wehzerwühlten, flammzerzuckten
Gramzerherbten Menschengesichtern.
Um sie forme ich
In vulkanischen Schöpfermächten
In purpurglutflackenden Krämpfen
All' weltauszusinnende
Gestaltende Gestaltungen
Wahnsinnsgeburten
Aus den Schattenklüften des All gegriffen
Gezerrt aus den Dunkelheiten der Feuerwelten
Meine mahnende Hand müht den Meissel.

Das Drama

Expressionism was essentially concerned more with the content of works of art than with the form. It is in this respect that it differs so fundamentally from neo-romanticism. In 1909 we find summed up in a few words of Sorge the change that was soon to come over the character of German literature when expressionism established itself. In November of that year Sorge notes:[1] "Vertiefung meiner Auffassung vom Werk des Lebens." The tendency of his thought from 1908 on could likewise be summed up in the words which he uses as the title for a short essay: *Über den Opfermut*.[2] He regarded, that is to say, his life as of value only in so far as he gave it to the service of humanity. This moral severity caused him to lose faith in the creations of his fellow-countrymen and to launch forth on a more earnest quest than that with which the neo-romantics had concerned themselves. He looked forward to a profound change in the life of mankind, for he regarded his own people as "voll nächtlicher Beschwernis."[3] That a change was approaching was not only his desire but his conviction. We find this idea expressed in language of a cosmic

[1] Tagebuch, MS.   [2] *So etwas wie Philosophie.*

[3] *Nachgelassene Gedichte*, herausgeg. von Martin Rockenbach, Leipzig, Vier Quellen Verlag, 1925.

intensity and suspense such as we find about the same
time in the work of Heym:

> Die in dem Tale wenden schon die Blicke
> Von Angst zerhöhet zu jenes Berges First,
> Wo schwere schwarze Wolke hoch gelagert
> Hockmütig thront, prunkend gehäuft zu Macht.
> Schon zucken Blitze ihre ersten Zeichen—
> Bald hebt ein Sturm den Staub der gelben Strassen
> In Nacht von Nebel und in erste Tropfen—
> Dann frisst der Strahl der Häuser niedre Spreu.[1]

About two months later he conceived the idea of a
new "Ich-Drama."[2] This later received the title *Der
Bettler* and represents the first important expressionist
work, from the appearance of which the beginning of
expressionism is often dated. Our investigations indicate, however, that when his complete works come to
be made public[3] it will be seen that expressionism took
root earlier than we had previously imagined.

[1] "Gewitter" (Symbolisch) 19/7/11, MS. It should be noted that it
was written before the appearance of George's *Stern des Bundes* and is
therefore independent of it.

[2] As he called it in the MS. of the I. Fassung.

[3] Their publication has already been planned. The date, however,
has been postponed.

CHAPTER IV

EXPRESSIONISM AND THE HELLENIC IDEAL

"It is an eternal and inexplicable dowry of the German people that at each spiritual awakening it remembers the Greeks, as if that which lies unborn within its own soul and which it wishes to express has once been represented in tangible form, and as if it had to develop its own individual qualities along the lines of this model which it discovers step by step."

FRIEDRICH WOLTERS in *Stefan George und die Blätter für die Kunst*.

THERE are few more striking features of literary history than the preoccupation of German poets with Greek literature and thought. Professor Butler has described in her work *The Tyranny of Greece over Germany* (Cambridge, 1935) the unrelenting fascination that Greece has exercised over German men of letters. In the preceding chapter we have seen how profoundly the expressionists were influenced by the Greeks in making their drastic changes in drama and stage. The purpose of this essay is to seek behind such external indications the spiritual kinship which the movement claimed with the mind of antiquity and in particular to observe its use of antique themes in order to set forth its own ideals and problems.

In 1912 Ludwig Curtius set out to answer the question: "What can antiquity mean to people of our time?"[1] He attacks the objective conception of Greece and asserts the need for an entirely subjective approach to Greek antiquity. After maintaining that true culture must express the individual spirit of a nation he goes on to say that we should not consider the Greeks merely historically nor romantically but as a people struggling with problems

[1] "Die Antike und wir" (*Jahrbuch d. Freien dt. Hochstifts*, Frankfurt, 1912).

50

similar to our own. In other words "antiquity is the mirror in which we recognise ourselves, our nature and the task of modern culture."

Parallel with this subjective interpretation of the past there developed, as a reaction against neo-romanticism, a movement away from the historical spirit.[1] The tendency to abandon historical restrictions opened up fruitful channels to the imagination, and the new possibilities thus revealed in the matter of treating old themes resulted in the writing of a considerable number of works based on subjects adapted from ancient myths. Another reason for the growth of interest in antique subjects can be found in the stimulus given by Nietzsche's insistence on the dionysiac aspect of Greek life and art.

The apolline view of Greece had predominated in Germany since Winckelmann in the eighteenth century defined the nature of Greek art as "noble simplicity and serene greatness." In 1872, however, Nietzsche's epoch-making work on *The Birth of Tragedy* stressed in Greek culture not the element of repose but that of wild passion. In contrast to Winckelmann he saw in Greek art not the expression of conscious self-control but that of a desperate and "tragic" wrestling with fate.

Nietzsche's interpretation was too challenging to receive immediate recognition, but the growth of spiritual and social unrest which culminated in the War years lent it an almost topical value and increased its influence. Indeed it became an essential part of the expressionist background.

Kurt Pinthus, editor of the expressionist anthology *Menschheitsdämmerung*, rejected the apolline conception of Greece when he wrote: "Even the statues of the Greeks do not—*pace* Winckelmann—aim at 'noble simplicity and serene greatness'"[2] and Wilhelm Michel, in depicting the expressionist view of life, resorts to this

---

[1] Cf. Kurt Wais: "Das Motiv des Vergangenen in der neueren Literatur" (*Vierteljahrsschr. f. Geistesgesch.-u. Lit. Wiss.*, Vol. X, 1932).

[2] In *Die Erhebung*, Berlin, 1919, Vol. I, p. 415 ff.

new dionysiac conception of Greece.[1] Michel defines his
idea of the "New Man" as one who feels anew the
"power of fate" and is overwhelmed by a "new sense of
cosmic laws." He then claims Hölderlin's authority
for his statement that the Germans lack the sense of fate.
He contrasts with the life of the ancients, as summed up
by Hölderlin, the attitude of his contemporaries to life.
"Heaven has lost its meaning for us, fate is deprived
of its significance and life has become untragic. We can
have happiness and unhappiness but not a 'fate.' There
are no longer any metaphysical horizons within our life."
With this outlook he contrasts again Hölderlin's comment
on the ancients that they were worthy "to stand in the
presence of the divine." "Everything in the world of
antiquity," says Michel, "was dynamic. The god invaded
life profoundly and with the strength of a storm. Hence
the possibility of the great tragic form in poetry and the
splendid development of man in the face of an overwhelming fate."

Expressionism in general was permeated by this
dionysiac view of life. The terms in which the expressionists speak of their "Weltanschauung" resemble closely the
manner in which Nietzsche speaks of Greece. When
Edschmid says that existence should consist of "perpetual
excitement" and that the artist's work should be "the
outburst of his inner self" we are at once reminded of
Nietzsche. The poets of the past whom the expressionists
most admire are those whose work reflects the dionysiac
outlook. In particular they felt a spiritual kinship to
Hölderlin. Michel published in 1920 an essay devoted
to him[2] which, although it purports to be a commentary
on the nature of Hölderlin's writing, is equally a statement of the expressionist point of view. Hölderlin's

[1] In *Der Mensch versagt*, Berlin, 1918, p. 48 ff. Michel's pamphlet is
one of the most important statements of policy of the expressionists.

[2] In the series "Die Silbergäule," Vol. XXXIII–XXXIIIa, Hanover,
1920; cf. also his essay on "Hölderlins Wiederkunft" (*Neue Rundschau*,
April, 1924).

Sophoclean fragments were re-edited by the expressionist Albert Ehrenstein and the poetry of Georg Trakl was deeply influenced by the work of Hölderlin. Dionysiac also was Hölderlin's contemporary, the dramatist Heinrich von Kleist, and Anselm Rust described *Penthesilea*, Kleist's tragedy dealing with the Queen of the Amazons, in the expressionist periodical *Die Aktion* (1911) as "the highest point of tragedy."[1]

It is therefore evident that the expressionists were not prepared to apply absolute standards of judgment to the classics. They regarded classicism not as an achievement to which ultimate value could be attributed, but as a phase to which one would not and could not return. Already in 1906 Wilhelm Worringer had written his *Abstraktion und Einfühlung* in which he sought to prove that art was necessarily only to be regarded as possessing significance relative to its age. Classicism, he claimed, was not one of the "absolute peaks of artistic creation." "All artistic production," Worringer concludes, "is nothing more than the continuous expression of the great struggle between man and matter which has been in progress since the creation and will continue until the end of time."

In the last stages of his work Worringer stresses the determining rôle played in art by intuition, and thus clinches an argument which is intended to demonstrate that art is essentially and inevitably subjective. This is indeed the foundation upon which all manifestations of expressionism are built. The doctrine of intuition—philosophically formulated by Bergson and Husserl and transferred by Freud to the sphere of psychology—plays a large part in expressionism; this becomes in consequence the literature of irrationalism. Here there is a curious paradox. The expressionist purports to be a seeker after absolute truths and yet he condemns himself to failure

---

[1] C. F. Reinhold in an article on "Kleist und der Expressionismus" (*Vossische Zeitung*, 18th September, 1919) declares that expressionist theories were anticipated in Kleist's theoretical writings such as *Brief eines jungen Dichters an einen jungen Maler.*

by his prepossession with his inner self. This paradox is illustrated by the hellenism of the expressionists, which necessarily treats Greek culture as of objective validity and yet subjectively reads into it the ideas of its own age.

In the years of transition, when the expressionist ideal was beginning to emerge from the whirlpool of spiritual currents in the first decade of the twentieth century, German literature was already concerned with Greek subjects. Paul Ernst, the most important figure in the neo-classical movement, wrote a series of dramas based on Greek subjects, beginning with *Demetrios* (1905). The work of Gerhart Hauptmann reveals a deep psychological affinity with the world of Greece,[1] even apart from his definitely neo-hellenic writings such as the *Griechischer Frühling* and the drama *Der Bogen des Odysseus* (1914). In these years also Carl Spitteler was occupied in writing his epic *Olympischer Frühling*, which appeared in final form in 1910. To the reader of Spitteler's splendid work it is clear that neo-hellenism was no longer merely an academic phase but the direct expression of exuberant feelings.

There are in particular two writers whose hellenism represents a stage in the pre-natal development of expressionism, Hugo von Hofmannsthal and Rudolf Pannwitz.

Of Hofmannsthal's four dramas on subjects borrowed from Greece we are concerned principally with the *Elektra* (1904). This play, a profound study in the power of hatred, is bathed in sombre colours and is the frenzied expression of elemental passion. One might apply to it the words of Michel: "Bright Apollo is dethroned. Dionysus is the god of the moment." In consequence, one critic described Hofmannsthal as the man who "pushed the theory of the dionysiac character of the Greeks to its logical conclusion." The content of his work was drawn from "the surging chaos of those

[1] Cf. F. A. Voigt, *Antike und antikes Lebensgefühl im Werke Hauptmanns*, Breslau, 1933.

tremendous myths, the home of all that is terrible, in which the most unheard of deeds are possible and where sense and madness are inseparably bound together."[1]

Rudolf Pannwitz was joint-editor with Otto zur Linde in 1904 of the pre-expressionist periodical *Charon*. He was much in the debt of Greek thought, indirectly through Nietzsche and directly through his enthusiasm for Heraclitus. He confessed his deep indebtedness to Nietzsche, for instance in his *Einführung in Nietzsche* (1920) and saw in him the reviver of the dionysiac religion of the Greeks.

Pannwitz' own aim was to give poetical expression to the ideas that Nietzsche had formulated philosophically. He attempted this in a number of *Mythen* as well as in several plays, the first five of which he edited under the collective title *Dionysische Tragödien*, written mainly between 1904 and 1910, published in 1913 and dedicated "to Nietzsche, the creator of our new life." These plays have never received as much attention as those of Hofmannsthal, probably because Pannwitz did not aim, like Hofmannsthal, at giving his versions of classical themes a modern character.

Pannwitz sets out to reconstruct the dionysiac form of antique drama in what he conceived to have been the original sense. For instance, in his "dionysiac tableau" *Die Befreiung des Oidipus* he introduces scenes of orgy as they are described by classical writers but were never performed on the stage as far as can be judged from extant Greek tragedy. Thus his plays have a predominantly historical character and the figures, such as Iphigenia, Empedocles, Croesus and Philoctetes, are to such an extent steeped in mysterious rites that they lack the interest which they arouse in ancient drama itself.

Nevertheless, it cannot be denied that in form and language Pannwitz foreshadows expressionism. He gives vent to restless emotion and he dissolves the form of the drama as is indicated by such sub-titles as "the Conclusion

[1] Lilli Hagelberg in the *Zeitschrift für Aesthetik*, XXVII, 1.

of a Tragedy" (*Der Tod des Empedokles*), a "Mystery Play" (*Philoktetes*), "an Event in Cantos and Five Scenes" (*Philolethes*) and "a Sacred Action in Three Circles" (*Orpheus*). His language resembles that of expressionism in its ecstatic utterances, its preference for ejaculation, the recurrent omission of parts of sentences and the tendency to attribute life to inanimate objects.

Thus the situation at the dawn of expressionism was that the dionysiac element prevailed in the attitude towards Greek antiquity in spite of an attempt by Paul Ernst to revive the apolline ideal. A direct link can thus be observed in this sphere between expressionism and the immediately preceding literary currents. It is therefore not surprising that Sorge, who represents the transitional period, was deeply concerned with the problem of Greek antiquity.

The divergence between the older and the expressionist generations in their attitude towards ancient Greece and its rôle in modern literature is reflected in Sorge's correspondence with Dehmel concerning his *Odysseus*. When he sent a copy to Dehmel it was returned unread. The latter had noticed an introductory remark to the effect that, although the costumes must in a general way resemble those of the Greeks, these must not be imitated in detail "since this work does not deal with the Greeks as such." Dehmel asked why, if the play was not concerned with Greece, this particular subject was chosen. The same policy, however, was pursued by Sorge a few months later when he wrote his *Prometheus* with similar intentions and discussed the question at some length. *Prometheus*, like *Odysseus*, presents an antique theme in modern guise but imbued with Greek elements. In *Odysseus* Nietzsche's idea of the Eternal Recurrence was used as the basis, and concerning *Prometheus* Sorge emphasised the fact that the Greek myth was radically altered by modern ideas but without losing its essential character in the process. From the particular he proceeded to the general and discussed the situation of literature in Germany with relation to the problem of which he had tentatively sought a solution in these two works. He found two kinds of drama at this time, the neo-romantic and the naturalist drama. The latter he regarded as sterile and incapable of further development. Neo-romantic drama, he considered, occupied itself too much with subjects drawn from the past while that of the naturalists went to the other extreme of an exaggerated actuality and realism. The future of literature will, like the former, be the heir of "a romantic classicism" but will imbue it with some of the realism of naturalism. *Prometheus*, which depicts the establishment on earth of a race of Nietzschean supermen, was offered as an example of what might be achieved along these lines.

Dehmel's position was not so far removed from that of Sorge as he imagined. *Odysseus* was not a case, as he thought, of an "aesthetic masquerade." On the contrary Sorge was seeking an answer to the very question with which Dehmel was concerned, the difficult problem of how to make use of an ancient theme in modern works without falling into the danger of sentimentality. Sorge evades the final difficulty involved in his attempts by leaving them as fragments without pushing them to their final conclusion of success or failure. Nevertheless his efforts in this sphere indicate that the question of the re-creation of themes borrowed from the past was urgent; a group of writers so relentlessly subjective as the expressionists could scarcely evade the difficulty. Sorge's attempts indicated the problems rather than provided a solution.

As expressionism developed further the attitude to antiquity became less compromising and more frankly subjective. The expressionists were more and more inspired by the desire not to lose themselves but to discover themselves in the past. Few writers illustrate this development so clearly as Georg Kaiser, whose play *Der Gerettete Alkibiades* (1920) bears directly on our subject. In this play it is not the Greek elements that

interest us so much as the light they throw on the author
and his attitude to them. Kaiser was one of the most
prolific dramatists of the period, and it is difficult to find
a formula to unite the multitudinous threads of the
forty-two dramas which he had published by 1938.
His approach to art, as is suggested by the title of
Diebold's monograph,[1] is predominantly intellectual. To
him "to write a drama is to work out an idea." Consequently the undefined lyricism and spiritual chiaroscura
of the majority of expressionists were alien to him. There
is further a Protean quality in his work that differentiates
him from many expressionists whose work is usually
unified and limited in scope. Kaiser has explained this
variety in his work in his description of the nature of the
drama as he sees it. "Drama," he says, "is a transition";
consequently "it is the duty of every creative artist to
turn away from each work."

If, therefore, we come to speak of one play of Kaiser we
must guard against the danger of drawing general conclusions from work that may have been consciously
superseded. Like all his plays *Der Gerettete Alkibiades* is
a "play with words," which for Kaiser constituted the
essence of wisdom. From this point of view comes his
admiration for what he described as "the drama of
Plato" which for him was "above all dramas." "Georg
Kaiser's *Geretteter Alkibiades*," wrote a critic, "was
derived from the mistaken idea that Plato's dialogues
were dramas" and it is pointed out that Klabund also
ranked Plato among the dramatists. "We have left the
sphere of mere contemplation," said Kaiser, "and have
entered the higher sphere in which we play with ideas."
It is possible to see a parallel between Kaiser's conception
of art and the dynamic nature of the expressionist
"Weltanschauung." "For not only the philosophy of the
expressionists," it has been said, "but also their poetics
are based on the fundamental idea of *movement*."[2]

[1] *Der Denkspieler Georg Kaiser*, Frankfurt, 1924.
[2] F. J. Schneider, *Der expressive Mensch und die deutsche Lyrik der
Gegenwart*, Stuttgart, 1927, p. 62.

The action of the play turns round two principal figures, Socrates and Alcibiades. Socrates is intellectually as astute as he is physically hindered. He is pre-eminently a man of thought and in this fact lies his strength. Alcibiades is his opposite. His talent lies exclusively on the physical side and by virtue of this fact he achieves distinction as a general. The play consists of an action which proceeds in the first place from complications that arise when Socrates unwittingly and by accident saves the life of Alcibiades and thereby secures the welfare of Athens. Socrates cannot rid himself of the trouble, the "thorn in his foot," which by chance had enabled him to save Alcibiades. The factor that was vital in the beginning must remain dominant until the end. By a kind of dramatic sophistry it leads to ideas and misunderstandings which in turn lead to higher truths. At the end of a story full of complications the conclusion that Kaiser draws is that death alone can unravel the ball, that "only Socrates can save Socrates—otherwise the world of Greece would collapse."

This work is not only the reflection of the outlook of an individual but also of an age. Expressionism was in many respects the child of an age of bustle and turmoil and mirrors the speed with which contemporary life moved. Kaiser formulates this connection when he says: "The aim of existence is to set up records, records in all spheres of life. The man of the highest achievement is the characteristic type of to-day," and Gustav Landauer emphasised, in an article devoted to Kaiser in the expressionist anthology *Die Gemeinschaft*, that Kaiser was "a man of our time." In Kaiser's view of life and art there is something of the restlessness and unresolved movement that is common to baroque and expressionism. Each of these tendencies grew up in an age that was shattered by war, the former by the Thirty Years' War and the latter by the Great War. It was as if Kaiser tried to compensate in this play for the loss of spiritual confidence by stressing unduly the rational element in life.

Much more convincing in his use of Greek themes was Franz Werfel, who "translated" the *Trojan Women* of Euripides under the title *Die Troerinnen.*[1] In the important preface Werfel says that he made the adaptation because he believed that "the history of mankind was once again passing through the situation from which Euripides' work originated." Euripides' work grew out of circumstances in the ancient world that resembled the background of expressionism. Just as the Great War was the supreme experience for the expressionists, so the war waged by Athens against the island of Melos was the background against which Euripides' play developed. This war, which led to the victory of Athens, produced in some circles in Greece much the same felling of revulsion as the Great War called forth in expressionist circles.[2]

In the Preface to the play Werfel discusses his interpretation of the subject as treated by Euripides and he reads into it his own expressionist ideas regarding life. Throughout his work in general Werfel is concerned with the idea that man alone can give meaning to the world. The creation is "inhuman" and "devoid of meaning"; thus Hecuba can speak of the "guilt of the Gods." Man is doomed, therefore, to suffer and this fact is "the most stupid stupidity of a mad world." Hecuba is to him the symbol of suffering thus caused, "the heaviest and poorest heart on earth."[3]

Werfel asks why Hecuba did not end her life by suicide. He finds the answer in the ethical principle that Man has not "the right to die," for only by living can he fulfil his duty of supplying the missing link in the chain of causality. Therefore "the duty of man is to live." Hecuba's duty is to fulfil her mission of "intermediary."

[1] First drafted in 1913 and published in *Die weissen Blätter.* It appeared in full in 1915 (Kurt Wolff Verlag, Leipzig).

[2] It may be noted that Clara Viebig used the same theme to express the desolation of war in her novel *Die Töchter der Hekuba,* 1917.

[3] From the poem *Hekuba*, composed as an epilogue to the play.

She is to be the "grosse Weltherz," the "grosse Welt-güte" of which Sorge speaks in *Der Bettler*.

The conclusion implied in Werfel's introductory discussion of the ideas of *Die Troerinnen* is that morality is better than happiness. Hecuba does not rejoice in her opportunity of sacrificing herself for her fellow creatures. It is only this fact, according to Werfel, that differentiates her from a Christian martyr. "The blood on Golgotha was not shed for her. She does not realise that, to be a saint, she need only transform her curses into jubilation." In other words she would have been in everything but name a Christian saint if for her passive resignation to her fate she had substituted a joyful acceptance.

Thus although Werfel kept closer to his original than the other expressionists who adapted Greek themes, new ideas have been grafted upon the model of Euripides. The many performances throughout Germany that followed the production at the Lessing Theatre in Berlin were greeted with tremendous enthusiasm; in the theme as presented by Werfel the public saw reflected their own sorrows and felt that in it their own age joined hands with the world of Greece.

Kurt Hiller, who was one of the leading activists and therefore not in sympathy with the passivity of Werfel's ethics as found in *Die Troerinnen*, published in his *Zur Ergänzung* an attack on Werfel.[1] The particular point at issue was Werfel's statement, referred to above, that Hecuba would have been a saint if her sufferings had produced a feeling of spiritual elation. Hiller objected that the better way would have been hostility and resistance, for since she accepted her suffering passively there was no chance of her improving her own lot and thereby of ameliorating the condition of the world. It was in reply to this that Werfel published his *Christliche Sendung* (1917). This document represents his final renunciation of activism, with which he had been in the past occasionally concerned.

[1] In *Tätiger Geist*, Munich, 1918.

As an activist Hiller was concerned with social reform,
whereas Werfel was occupied with the things of the spirit.
To Hiller it was the social progress of the masses that
mattered; Werfel was concerned with the spiritual salvation of the individual. The community that Werfel envisaged was one of the spirit, where the individual could
develop his individuality to the full; that to which Hiller
looked forward meant the absorption of the individual by
the masses, whose social welfare was his main thought.
"Mankind can only be saved," wrote Hiller, "at the cost
of sacrificing the individual." This idea is alien to *Die
Troerinnen*, but it is fundamental to Hasenclever's
Antigone.

Antigone, like *Die Troerinnen*, plays against the background of war. Whereas Werfel is concerned with the
moral aspect of the situation, Hasenclever is interested
predominantly in its social implications. Werfel's treatment of his theme has, it is true, a topical application but
not to the same degree as that of Hasenclever, who in his
play portrays the political world of his time under the
cloak of an antique theme. There is, for example, little
doubt that Creon is intended as a satirical picture of the
German Emperor.

The difference between the two plays is reflected in the
language. Werfel, interested in the gentler emotions of
the soul, uses a style that is softer and sweeter than that of
Hasenclever, whose aim is to drive home ideas of social
upheaval. Therefore, his language is hard and matter-of-
fact, beaten out into steely sentences which succeed each
other like blows of a hammer. Werfel was writing as a
poet, Hasenclever as a preacher. The following passages
illustrate the difference. Typical of Werfel's *Die
Troerinnen* are the lines:

ANDROMACHE

Wir rufen vermessen die Toten, sie gleiten an dumpfen Gestaden,
Leben ist Jammer—auf uns stürzt die zertrümmerte Stadt.
In unendlichem Zug umschreiten uns Larven des Leidens.
Zorn der Götter, geballt, grinst aus dem Drang des Gewölks.

Paris, dein sündiger Sohn, er lockte das Schicksal von oben,
Nun in Athenas Hain modern die Leichen verkrallt.
Raben wie Zunder des Brands umflattern die schreckliche Stätte,
Doch wer vom Volke noch lebt, hockt und wartet der Fahrt.

HEKUBA

Land des Lebens, du Heimat, o Stadt am Himmel gestürzte!
Haus, wo ich Stolze die Zahl strahlender Kinder gebar!
Kinder, wo riss es euch hin . . . nicht hält mehr zu atmender Nachtzeit
Lind die Mutter das Licht euch über Schlummer und Traum.
Nur den Lebenden bleibt die steigende Sintflut der Tränen,
Aber die Toten sanft lächeln im Lichte des Nichts.

CHÖRE

Tränen, unendliche Tränen, es blühen die Wüsten der Qualen
Stürzt in das brennende Aug' süss das Gewässer der Welt.

Hasenclever's *Antigone* opens with the following lines spoken by the Herald:

Der Krieg ist aus.   Die Feinde sind geschlagen.
Die Stadt ist frei.
Eteokles, der König, fiel
Im Zweikampf mit dem Bruder Polyneikes;
Beide kamen grässlich um durchs Schwert.
Eteokles ist tot.   Kreon ist König.
Kreon befiehlt:
Die Leichen der Gefallenen zu begraben;
Freudenfeuer, Gottesdienst
Zu feiern für die Rettung unsrer Heimat.
Man gebe dem Eteokles ein Grab,
Ein königliches Grab,
Würdig seiner Asche: Held und Retter.
Doch Polyneikes, der Verräter, giftige Saat
Vom Schatten des Ödipus, der mit dem Zug
Der Sieben gegen Theben zog, die Herrschaft
An sich zu reissen—bleibt liegen
Dort auf dem Schlachtfeld, Hund—und Vogelbeute.
Zum Himmel stinkt sein faules Aas,
Denkmal der Schande allen Menschen,
Kreon befiehlt:
Wer des Verbotes ungeheure Mahnung
Übertritt—
Wer dieser Leiche letzte Ehre spendet,
Der wird zu Tod gesteinigt,
Sein Kadaver jedem zugestellt.
So rächen wir die Taten unsrer Feinde!

In *Die Troerinnen* Hecuba forms the central kernel of the play and the problems that Werfel raises are those that concern individuals. Above all he is concerned with the question of what should be the ethical attitude of the individual in the face of a social upheaval such as war. The central point of *Antigone* on the other hand is the Crowd, which appears either as an entity or in one of its subdivisions, represented by "the Man from the Crowd," "an Old Lady," "a Blind Man," etc. The Crowd occupies as the play progresses an increasingly large portion of the action; when the action reaches its climax in the last act, the Crowd has the stage almost to itself.

The importance that the expressionist attached to the idea of communal life brings the expressionist drama close in its general character to the drama of Greece with its prominent chorus. Thus it tried to rectify what Iwan Goll criticised as a defect in modern drama which, he said, dealt only with the individual and not with man in general and in which he found no crowd scenes that equalled the power of the ancient chorus.

To return to Hasenclever's play. Antigone, nominally the heroine, is hardly more than the voice of the people. It is to her that we must look to discover the views that Hasenclever wishes so forcibly to impress upon us. She ultimately determines the future of the people, and it is to her that they look for their salvation. Hecuba had not attempted to bring about any outward form of amelioration. Hers had been in the first place a moral task. Antigone, however, is concerned with external realities. She is an active personality in contrast to Hecuba whose nature and virtue lie in her passivity. When in the last act the King and Queen withdraw from their high office and, at her instigation, dedicate themselves to the welfare of the people, her mission is accomplished. The various stages of Antigone's success stand out clearly; her exchange of opinion with the crowd in the second act, her description in the same act of the vision whereby her pity for mankind was first awakened and, in the third act, her discussion with Hæmon, his conversion and finally her conversion of Creon.

Antigone is a plea for radical socialism and it is significant that it appeared in 1917, the year of the Russian Revolution. It preaches the need for a new life based on the brotherhood of man. Antigone is "the first creature of the New World," and the play is a plea for pacifism in a time distracted by war. "War passes away; nations offer the hand of friendship" is the comment of a member of the Crowd at the end of *Antigone*. Words from a contemporary review of Gertrud Fauth's play *Agamemnon* could be applied to *Antigone*: "The people speaks with the voice of our years of war. It utters lamentations for sons and husbands; it incites to revolution; it cries for bread and reconciliation."[1] As Goll in his *Dithyramben* (1918) used the Golden Fleece as a symbol of peace, so Hasenclever gives expression to his pacifism within the framework of a Greek story. Thus Hasenclever's version leads from the problems of ancient Greece to the urgent questions of twentieth-century life. Moreover, like Werfel, he superimposes on the Greek legend the terminology of Christian religion. Antigone regards her task as a religious obligation; she sacrifices herself in accordance with what she believes to be God's decree:

> Gott!
> Lass mich am Sarge des Bruders
> Zur Gnade schweben.

Likewise the King considers himself responsible directly to God:

> Gott gab mir Majestät,
> Dass ich euch würdig führe.
> Ihm allein schuld ich Rechenschaft.

The "Voice from the Grave" says at the close of the play:

> Volk,
> Falle nieder—
> Gott hat gerichtet

and thus the drama ends, like *Die Troerinnen*, with the

[1] Cf. *Das Literarische Echo*, 1920–21, p. 423

introduction into the Greek theme of religion in the
Christian sense.[1] This combination of the pre-Christian
and Christian world is found also in Josef Winckler's
volume of poems *Der Irrgarten Gottes* (1922) which
depicts the entry of Christ just before His Passion into
Olympus. From Prometheus he discovers that mankind
does not wish to be redeemed. It will be shown in a later
chapter how expressionist religious experience represents
a strange mixture of orthodox Christianity with elements
suggestive of nature-religion. One is reminded of the
words of Rudolf Kayser in 1920: "The lyrical poetry of
our time bravely endeavours to reach God. The God that
it seeks is at once a heathen deity and the Christian God."[2]

It is a far cry from the political reasoning of *Antigone*
to the dionysiac fury of Oskar Kokoschka's two plays on
Greek subjects, *Mörder, Hoffnung der Frauen* (1907) and
Orpheus und Eurydike (1918). In these he dealt with the
problem—which had already attained a topical interest—
of the relation of the sexes. His approach to this problem
was not, as with Freud, psychological, but elemental.
Kokoschka dealt with experiences that lie outside the pale
of rational life and accordingly his plays lack even the
semblance of logical development. The characters in
Mörder Hoffnung der Frauen are driven by elemental
passion and by "mad desire from horror to horror." Thus
at the order of the man, who is the main figure, the
warriors are ready to torture the woman, and she, in a
manner befitting the character of the Amazons with
whom the story is concerned, returns the attack. He is
indeed a wild animal, as she calls him, but towards the
end of the play the mystery of the extraordinary events
reveals itself to him. "Dark things become clear" to him
when the woman reveals that she is his wife. The same
struggle between the sexes is the subject of *Orpheus und
Eurydike*, the scene of which is set in the Underworld—

[1] Cf. Rosa Daxlberger, *Der Heilige in der deutschen Dichtung*, Munich,
1937, pp. 62 ff.
[2] Cf. D. W. Schumann, *Germanic Review*, IX (1933), p. 60.

a circumstance that alone is sufficient to rob the play of any semblance of reality. Figures from Hades appear on the stage and Charon's bark is seen. The symbolism to which Kokoschka resorts makes a rational approach to to the play impossible and the wild dance of the women round Orpheus may be taken as characteristic of a play whose ultimate purpose would seem to be to display all the animal instincts of humanity.[1] The hellenism of the expressionists reached even more startling extremes in Becker's *Das Letzte Gericht* where the Gods of Greece bow down before an idol symbolising capitalism.

Two representatives of Greek mythology and philosophy respectively, Prometheus and Heraclitus, attracted only the casual attention of the expressionists although they corresponded closely to their own ideas.

It is strange that, apart from Sorge, Heynicke was almost alone in making Prometheus the subject of his work, for it might have been expected that the activists would have seen in his defiance the embodiment of their ideals. In Heynicke's poem *Prometheus*, however, the hero's promise to establish on earth a celestial garden in which to celebrate voluptuous festivals is in direct contrast to the spirit of activism. But we have the authority of Max Picard that the movement recognised its kinship to the active ideals of Hercules.

The neglect of Prometheus by the expressionists is no less striking than the scarcity of their references to Heraclitus, whose thought stands close to the ideas both of neo-romanticism[2] and expressionism. His conception of life as unceasing movement forms a parallel to the

---

[1] It may here be noted that the same subject is found in Gerrit Engelke's poem *Eurydike* (*Rhythmus des Neuen Europa*, p. 80) and the Orpheus legend was adapted by Iwan Goll in *Der Neue Orpheus. Eine Dithryambe*, Munich, 1918.

[2] Especially as represented by Hofmannsthal, cf. J. Sofer, *Die Welt-theater Hugo von Hofmannsthals und ihre Voraussetzungen bei Heraklit und Calderon*, Vienna, 1934.

expressionist emphasis on the dynamic element, "das biologisch Bewegte."[1]

Heynicke speaks in Heraclitean tones when he describes himself as "a human being in the arms of eternal development":

> Werde!
> Aufjubelnde Seele des All!
> Ich bin ein Mensch im Arme des ewigen Werdens,
> Geheimnis ist selig erschlossen,
> ich bin in mich selber hell ausgegossen,
> mit blauem Riesenfittich schweb ich gen Sonne!

and Wilhelm Klemm approaches still more closely the ideas of the Ephesian philosopher when he formulates his conception of the world as in a state of flux:

> Was uns Endlichen als Welt entgegenströmt;
> Will ich fassen in sterbliche Worte.

When Edschmid proclaimed that expressionist art was alive with "movement," he could have found an authoritative precedent in the treatise *Concerning Nature* for the expressionists, among whom only Pannwitz acknowledged a debt to Heraclitus.

With the expressionists Hellenism became an outlet for many of their most characteristic ideas. Even a short work like Becher's *Ikaros*[2] is a mosaic of typical utterances, based on the fundamental expressionist belief in the indestructibility of "Geist." Each aspect of the movement found support in ancient Greece. The rational current in expressionism, represented by Hiller, Kaiser and Hasenclever, was in a sense a rebirth of the Platonic element of pure reason, while the irrational current is reflected in Goll's emphasis on the "boundless passion" of Greek drama and in Lothar Schreyer's praise of Aeschylus at the expense of Euripides.

[1] Cf. Carl Einstein, *Die Kunst des* 20. *Jahrhunderts*, Propyläen-Kunstgeschichte. Berlin, 1931, p. 13.
[2] In *Die Erhebung I.*

It is particularly interesting to observe that, just as the expressionists had sought to justify their ideas by reference to Greece, so too the reaction that followed the decline of the movement sought authority in Greece for its tenets. Eugen Diesel in his *Der Weg durch das Wirrsal* (1926) attacked the abstractness of expressionism and contrasted it with the "naturalness" of the Greeks. Similarly Johst in 1924 was repelled by the lack of self-discipline in expressionism and opposed to it the restraint of the Greeks. With the return in Germany to a new spirit of order and discipline came a more orthodox hellenism. In 1931, for example, we find the Austrian writer Max Mell in his play *Die Sieben gegen Theben* treating the Greek original in a spirit of reverence rather than experiment.

The year in which Mell's play was published witnessed the appearance of Eugene O'Neill's drama *Mourning becomes Electra*, which had been begun in 1926. O'Neill's treatment of his subject is largely expressionist, and a German critic[1] has gone so far as to describe this play as "the most important attempt of expressionism to deal with an antique theme." The form of the drama, with its fourteen scenes which succeed each other in breathless sequence, its preoccupation with the elemental forces of life, its treatment of individuals as types stripped of their individual characteristics, its background of a ghost-like reality and its themes of madness, passion, conflict and relentless Fate,—all these features indicate O'Neill's relationship to expressionism.

The hellenism of the expressionists was intensely subjective, concerned with problems which ancient Greece never envisaged, with riddles of death Thebes never knew. During expressionism the tyranny of Greece over Germany's intellectual life was maintained, though with less rigour than in the serener age of Winckelmann and Goethe. In the eighteenth century Greece had represented

---

[1] Cf. Friedrich Brie, "Eugene O'Neill als Nachfolger der Griechen" in the *Germanisch-Romanische Monatsschrift*, 1933.

to German poets the embodiment of earthly beauty and joy, but the expressionists, stimulated by Nietzsche and straining eagerly towards a transcendental reality, found in it the expression of

> Infinite passion, and the pain
> Of finite hearts that yearn.

CHAPTER V

FRANZ KAFKA AND SÖREN KIERKEGAARD

IN the years immediately preceding the War a new spirit began to assert itself in German literature and art and gradually to claim for itself the name of expressionism (Ausdruckskunst). Whereas the impressionists—which term is here applied especially to the neo-romantics—had aimed at reproducing the *impression* which the world made upon them, the expressionists tried to *express* the underlying idea of all phenomena. Expressionism was in consequence not concerned with verisimilitude, and in its burning desire to discover what it believed to be the essentials it often cultivated the grotesque and the fantastic. As far as literature is concerned it may be said to have come into recognition with the publication in 1912 of Reinhard Johannes Sorge's play *Der Bettler*.

Expressionism may in part be explained as a reaction against the non-creative, receptive aspect of impressionism but it would be false to regard it as its exact opposite. Indeed the neo-romantic writers, in so far as they recalled men to the claims of imagination and of the supersensual, may be said to have prepared the way for the spiritual awareness which constitutes the religious aspect of expressionism.

To this spiritual preparation must be added the influence of the War which was largely responsible for bringing expressionism to its climax. The War, by putting men face to face with death and destruction, made them conscious of the need to establish their lives on something more than a basis of material reality. Expressionism was in consequence strongly religious, but in no settled or orthodox fashion. Expressionist religion was metaphysical rather than confessional. Its God was a vague cosmic force rather than a personal deity. Further, expressionist religion was a quest rather than a fulfilment. Thus André Gide, who exercised a strong influence on the period, is at one with the expressionists when he describes his view of religion as "un rapprochement infini" and not "une confusion en Dieu" (*Les Nourritures Terrestres*). Much expressionist literature is rhapsodic and formless; that this is not necessarily the case is shown by the work of Franz Kafka.

Kafka, though he was clearly linked up with expressionist thought, stood outside the expressionist circle and differs from the expressionists in being more closely bound to the past. Moreover he was a writer who possessed greater originality than the majority of those in the expressionist school. Kafka was born in Prague in 1883 and came of a well-to-do Jewish family. After studying law at the German University in Prague he became a clerk in an insurance company. An unhappy love affair weakened his constitution and undermined his courage for life. Early in the War he experienced the first traces of consumption and went in the course of time to several sanatoria. In 1923 he went to Berlin where he suffered from malnutrition at the time of the deepest economic distress in Germany. He married in the same year, but he was already a hopeless invalid. He died the following year.

Kafka's work has had a curious fate. He himself published only a few short stories and he was always reluctant to hand his writings over to the public. He destroyed many of his works and, in his will, he ordered that all his papers should be burned. A portrait of Kafka has been drawn by Max Brod in his novel *Kingdom of Love* (*Zauberreich der Liebe*) London 1930, in the character of Richard Gerta. Kafka's intellectual ancestors are to be found in Kierkegaard, whose spiritual position he recognised as similar to his own, and in Pascal. His style is simple and his language translucently clear. Even the occasional intrusion of the grotesque is camouflaged by the quietness and verisimilitude of his style. In reading Kafka indeed one is reminded of the older impressionist German literature. The collection of short passages which bear the title *Observations* (*Betrachtung*) seems in some respects to belong to the same tradition as the work of Peter Altenberg, who may be regarded as the typical impressionist.

Nevertheless Kafka's world of apparently simple reality has a special symbolical and mystical significance. He depicts side by side, as it were, two distinct worlds. The first is the world of earthbound reality, as can be seen from the titles of some of the pieces in *Betrachtung*. Thus he describes here "Kinder auf der Landstrasse," "Der Ausflug ins Gebirge," "Das Unglück der Junggesellen," "Kleider," etc. The other is the world of metaphysical speculation at which he often hints even in his treatment of the simple things of workaday life. He even went so far as to maintain that the spiritual world alone was the real world, and that that, which we call the world of the senses, was but an element of the spirit of evil that had invaded the world of the spirit. It is in this respect that the difference between impressionism and expressionism is especially clearly seen; it has rightly been said that, whereas a man like Altenberg transfers the external world into himself, Kafka translates his inner self into the world of objectivity; he does this by discovering between the ego and the world yet another "being," namely the human being who is in a condition in which he is no longer himself, but in which he is not yet the "other being." Cysarz has this same idea in mind when he defines Kafka's work as "the embodiment of the higher and the lower world in a world of concrete existence."

In his exercise of this mystical second-sight Kafka is the full expressionist. Here the influence of Dostoevsky must be recognised on the movement. One of the main contributions that Dostoevsky made to expressionism was that he established a world of metaphysical reality distinct from that of finite existence. It is, for example, in this higher world that Ivan (in *The Brothers Karamasov*) lives. The problem of reconciling the two is treated in *Crime and Punishment*. It is the struggle that takes place in Raskolnikoff's conscience.

Kafka searches, like many expressionists, for a spiritual reorientation. Even before the War German poets had begun to proclaim the hollowness of the life they saw around them. Heym, Stadler and Trakl may be mentioned as three writers who, standing on the threshold of expressionism, were not blinded by the apparent outward prosperity of the pre-War years, but were conscious of the inner instability of this time. Kafka, who was thirty-one when the War broke out, was older than the majority of the expressionists, and thus the world of reality, which even before the War had undergone a change, lost its meaning entirely for his generation. Man's relationship to God appeared to be severed. Man was thrown back upon himself and was set the task of establishing his life upon a new basis. This search for new foundations is the quest of the expressionists and is the subject of Kafka's work. He seeks to reconcile the finite and the infinite.

His work is symbolical because his aim is to express the infinite in finite terms. He even succeeds in imparting to his writing a note of quiet simplicity when he is dealing with transcendental considerations. This characteristic is seen clearly in the short story called *Die Verwandlung*, which was begun in 1912 and published in 1916. A commercial traveller awakes one morning to find that he has turned into a monster. Thus at once we are presented with a situation grotesque in the extreme. Yet Kafka succeeds in maintaining an atmosphere of probability throughout. The circumstances in which the action develops are taken from everyday life. Gregor Samsa, the unfortunate central figure, his father, mother and sister are depicted in their home. We are introduced to the

common problems of the housewife and to the affairs
of a small business house. Yet over all hangs the impossible fate of Gregor Samsa. On the face of it, merely
a sombre domestic tragedy. Nevertheless the story has a
deeper note. The sudden change in Samsa is to be
regarded as the symbolical presentation of the dissolution
of the prevailing order of things, such as took place under
the impact of the War. Man must reckon with new and
revolutionary values, just as Samsa must change his
whole existence and adapt himself to the circumstances
arising out of his new condition. *Die Verwandlung* is a
significant document of the War period.

The full extent of Kafka's "Weltanschauung" is found
in the novels, all of which were published after his death.
Der Prozess, *Das Schloss*, and *Amerika* are nominally
separate works, though in point of fact they form a
trilogy. They depict the search of an individual for an
order of life which will satisfy his needs. These quests are
the symbolical representation, as Max Brod points out,
of the craving for "admission to a kingdom of God" and
indicate, in the words of Naumann, "the way to God."
In each case, with the possible exception of *Amerika*, of
which the last chapter is not completed, the search is
vain; the action shows the hero apparently coming nearer
to his goal but in the end he is as far from it as ever.

For example, in *Der Prozess* (which was begun in
1914), we have the story of a bank-manager unjustly
accused. His professional life is ruined. He seeks to
prove his innocence and takes measures which he hopes
will lead to his acquittal. Yet he never succeeds in
reaching the representatives of the Law, who are depicted
as being protected by a maze of impenetrable formulae.
Even his own lawyer is idle and inefficient. The law-
courts are housed in disreputable buildings which are
only accessible by endless staircases leading to ante-
rooms, and not to the offices where the officials work,
whom he seeks. He never finds the fulfilment for which
he is looking, and the final chapter, behind which lurks

an air of grotesque unreality, ends on a note of despair: "Who was it? A friend? A good man? One who would help him? Was it a single individual? Were there many? Was there still help? Was there evidence that had been overlooked? Certainly there was. Even unshakeable logic may yield to the man who is fighting for his life. Where was the judge whom he had never seen, and where was the High Court of Justice to which he had never been admitted? He stretched out his open hands in despair."

Similarly *Das Schloss* is a story of frustration. It relates to a surveyor who arrives at the Castle to take up duties which he believes await him there. His efforts to enter upon the duties for which he has been nominated lead him from one official to another. The officials to whom he is admitted prove to have only very subordinate authority. He discovers finally from the Superintendent that his appointment was an error since there is no room in the organisation of the Castle for another surveyor. His quest has led him nowhere.

Thus for all their quiet everyday narrative form the plots of these novels might have been transferred from troubled dreams. We need not postulate the influence of Freud on expressionism, although it is interesting to note that Mr. Day Lewis, in his *Revolution in Writing*, mentions Kafka among the authors most admired by the young writers of to-day precisely because of his Freudian introspection. The symbolism of dreams, however, has been a commonplace of religious experience in all ages.

The last novel of the group is *Amerika*. Although chronologically it precedes the other two (it was begun in 1912) it must be regarded, by virtue of its content, as following upon them. For in this work Kafka suggests the possibility of a happy ending of fulfilment, and thus it stands apart from most of his work. Only in one other work does Kafka offer a similar prospect, namely in the short piece entitled *Der Bau*. This was one of his last works, written at the end of his life, at the time when he had at last found domestic happiness. The fundamental note of his work is nevertheless resignation and renunciation. Here he is in line with his fellow expressionists. For all their apparently buoyant optimism they often felt, deep down in themselves, that their ideals would never be fulfilled. It is perhaps significant in this connection that several of their important works remained unfinished. One thinks for example, of Fritz von Unruh's proposed trilogy, of which the third volume, for which *Ein Geschlecht* and *Platz* were the preparation, was never written. One might mention too the essentially fragmentary nature of almost all Kafka's work. With him it seems to have been almost a habit to flinch from the final step. *Der Prozess*, *Das Schloss* and *Amerika* all lack conclusions.

This inability to push ideas to their logical conclusion is symptomatic of a fundamental weakness in expressionism. This weakness is seen clearly in the religious outlook of the expressionists and in particular in Kafka's work. Expressionism suffered from the irreconcilable duality of the finite and the infinite. The expressionists stressed the infinite as the corner-stone of the New World to which they looked forward; their cry was always for "Ewigkeit." Yet infinity by its very nature excludes fulfilment. Werfel, who was one of the leading expressionists, recognised this fact when he exclaimed in his *Bocksgesang* that "all eternity flees from fulfilment." Kafka also has this idea when he says in one of his recently published aphorisms: "He who seeks never finds." The freedom that they so vehemently demanded as part of their spiritual programme was illusory from the beginning, although they were loath to admit it. Like Kafka's heroes the expressionists were unable to reach the goal that they had set themselves. "The ideal of freedom," says Kafka, "is too often deceptive," and he confessed to a "feeling of the most complete helplessness." This organic weakness in the constitution of the expressionist "Weltanschauung" accounts, just as much as the unfavourable economic and social circumstances in Germany after the War, for the collapse of the movement about 1924. There is in consequence a note of negation in much expressionist literature and, in the case of Kafka, this takes on a religious colouring. Kafka sums this up when he says: "Heaven is silent to our entreaties." The conclusion at which Kafka hints with despairing persistence is that, before God, man is always in the wrong. "Everything," he remarked on one occasion, "is but deception." Max Brod has stressed the fact that behind the novels of Kafka lies the search for divine grace. Kafka's characters, however hard they strive to this end, never reach it. Kafka is in this respect characteristic of expressionism. The value of expressionism lies, not so much in what it actually achieved, as in the beginning that it opened up to others. It was the tragedy of these writers that they could not themselves progress along the path that they had discovered; it was their greatness that they felt this tragedy deeply, and their contribution that they prepared the way for others.

In a notice in his diary Kafka says that he "represents the negative aspect" of his age. He adds that he has not the same degree of religious support as Kierkegaard. In point of fact Kafka stood very close to the spiritual position of Kierkegaard, as he himself recognised. Kierkegaard's work had been published in Denmark in the middle of the nineteenth century, but it was not until the first decade of the twentieth century that he was discovered so far as Germany was concerned. Kafka was drawn to the thought of Kierkegaard since the latter had been pre-occupied with precisely that problem which underlies Kafka's work in particular and expressionist religious experience in general, that is to say, the problem of the relationship of the finite individual to the world of infinity. It will therefore cast a valuable light on this examination of expressionist religion to survey the relationship of Kafka to the philosophy of Kierkegaard. In 1913 he records the view that Kierkegaard's outlook is "despite

important differences" very similar to his own. Further
it is known that he studied *Furcht und Zittern*[1] in great
detail. The letters to his friend, Robert Klopstock,
include a discussion of the argument of this work. He
devoted several of his aphorisms to points that interested
him in the philosophy of Kierkegaard.

The parallel that exists between Kafka and Kierkegaard
seems to extend even to the lives of the two men. Kierkegaard was born during the period of romanticism;
Kafka was born shortly before the revival of romantic
ideas in Germany. In the centre of the life of each stands
the breaking off of an engagement, events which in both
cases had profound repercussions on their thought and
writing. Both were in the main free-lance writers; the
words of Kierkegaard: "My delight is to think, writing
represents my real life," might equally be applied to
Kafka. Finally both dies at a comparatively early age.

The style of both men has a curious indirectness.
Kierkegaard, in his *Unwissenschaftliche Nachschrift*
describes his method as "indirect information." That is to
say, the reader has the impression that a third person
stands between himself and Kierkegaard. Kafka likewise
adopts an "indirect" method, but of a different type;
his characters exist not in their own right but as representatives of two worlds. They are the embodiment of
the higher and lower in a world of concrete existence.

Kafka's characters, therefore, are faced with one overwhelming problem; they must reconcile the finite and the
infinite. This is, of course, the same problem that con-
fronted Sorge in *Der Bettler*. They are finite creatures
whose task is to fulfil transcendental obligations. Thus
there is a dualism in Kafka's work that excludes fulfilment.
It has been pointed out by a writer on Kierkegaard that
the words "in the eyes of God" recur in his writing with
striking frequency.[2] The problem of adapting one's life

[1] In the absence of English translations, reference is made to the titles
of German translations.

[2] W. Ruttenbeck, *Sören Kierkegaard, der christliche Denker und sein
Werk*, Berlin, 1929.

to the claims of both worlds stood in the forefront of
Kierkegaard's thought. It is the problem of what he
calls "Existence." This aspect of his work has been
defined thus: "The man who 'exists' is to him (Kierkegaard) the man who stands in a fundamental relationship
to the world and to God; or, more exactly, the man who
stands in a relationship to God and who expresses this
relationship in his relationship to the world."[1] Max Brod
has stressed the point that Kafka was preoccupied with
the idea that it was impossible for man to fulfil the will of
God; man must necessarily be in the wrong. Similarly
Kierkegaard speaks of his feeling of "responsibility to
eternity." Kafka expresses this consciousness of the
overpowering task of justifying his finite existence by the
standards of the infinite. "What is oppressive in the
conception of eternity," he says, "is the justification
which we cannot understand, that time, and consequently
we ourselves, must experience by the standards of
eternity." In his diary Kierkegaard says: "In my conscience God has cast His eyes upon me and it is impossible
for me to forget that His eye is watching me." Kafka
speaks similarly when he proclaims the oppressive
thought of eternity: "I ought to welcome eternity and
yet, when I find it, I am sad. I ought to feel myself
perfect through eternity and yet I feel oppressed."

We constantly come across reflections in Kafka's work
about the insufficiency of merely recognising the right
course and the obligation to act in accordance with it.
Here we meet the problem that Kierkegaard formulated
under the term "Existence." Thus Kafka says: "Nobody
can be content with moral perception in the abstract;
one must act in accordance with it." Again he maintains that the verb "to be" has a double meaning: it
means "to exist" and also "to belong to God." He
sums up the problem when he says: "Man is a free
and assured citizen of the earth, for he is attached to a

[1] Cf. B. Meerpohl, *Die Verzweiflung als metaphysisches Phänomen in
der Philosophie S. Kierkegaards*, 1934.

chain that is long enough to allow him to move in all
the spaces of the earth; but its length is such that nothing
can draw him beyond the boundary of the earth. At the
same time, however, he is a free and assured citizen of
Heaven, for he is likewise attached to a heavenly chain of
corresponding length. If he wishes to come to earth, he
is throttled by the heavenly noose; if he wishes to enter
Heaven he is throttled by the earthly noose."

In Kierkegaard's view man is linked to God by his
conscience. By recognising the fact of conscience, man has
eternity within him; it is his point of contact with God.
"However terrible it is to have even the slightest thing on
one's conscience, through this link with God everything
receives tremendous importance," Kierkegaard says in
the *Erbauliche Reden*. By reason of this link with eternity
man can never utterly destroy himself. This fact was a
source of perpetual disquiet to him. Thus he complains
that "he cannot annihilate himself, cannot get rid of
himself, cannot reduce himself to nothing." Similarly
Kafka speaks of death as merely "an apparent end" and
regrets "the mystery of the impossibility of annihilation."
"Each individual is indestructible," he says, "and
indestructibility is a quality common to us all."

Faced by these problems and responsibilities man is
depicted by Kierkegaard and Kafka as utterly alone. He
must solve his problems unaided by outside help.
Meerpohl sums up this aspect of Kierkegaard's thought:
"No human community can help him to bear the burden
that God has imposed upon him." Man hovers, in
Kierkegaard's words, "over an abyss of 70,000 feet,
many many miles away from all human help." Kafka's
three novels have aptly been described as "a trilogy of
loneliness." His hero seeks but never finds help from his
fellow men, and this feeling of desertion finds particularly
poignant expression at the close of *The Trial*. He
lamented the fact that only rarely had he been able to
enter "the territory between loneliness and intercourse"
and he complained that his age lacked "religious com-

munal life." He was a "deserted soul" flitting "around the house of life."

These parallelisms between the ideas of Kafka and those of Kierkegaard are striking. Fundamentally both men stand on common ground. The spiritual uneasiness of both emanates from what Kierkegaard calls "despair at infinity." It was not that Kierkegaard determined the course of Kafka's thought, but he strengthened it. Thus in recording his early impressions of Kierkegaard, Kafka writes: "He confirms my ideas like a friend."

The work of Kafka is the most characteristic manifestation of the fundamental problem of the expressionists' struggle towards God. The expressionists, emphasising now man's earthly heritage of joy and sorrow, now the destiny that awaits him in the transcendental world, brought themselves face to face with the mutually exclusive claims of the finite and the infinite. No other religious writer of expressionism grappled so relentlessly with this problem, and in the work of no other expressionist is the impossibility of its solution, at any rate upon an expressionist basis, more clearly revealed.[1] For the answer which Kafka sought in Kierkegaard could only be furnished by a middle course, and the expressionists, paying the penalty of too great zeal, were constitutionally ill-fitted to compromise. It is noteworthy than an answer was suggested in these years by a poet of an earlier generation who stood outside the expressionist circle, but was not untouched by its influence. In the *Duineser Elegien*,[2] which of all Rilke's works is that on which the imprint of expressionist ideas is most clearly

---

[1] *Pace* Max Brod, Kafka's close friend, who in his *Franz Kafka. Eine Biographie (Erinnerungen und Dokumente)*, Prague, 1937, denies that Kafka's "Weltanschauung" was one of despair. Brod's subjective and biassed view of Kafka is summed up by R. Wellek in his review of Brod's Book in *Scrutiny*, June, 1938, pp. 86–9.

[2] For treatment in English of the Elegies, cf. the essay by E. L. Stahl, in *Rainer Maria Rilke. Aspects of his Mind and Work*. Ed. by W. Rose and G. Craig Houston; London, 1938.

seen, Rilke sought an answer to the same problem, and in the figure of the "angels," as later in the "double-kingdom" of the *Sonette an Orpheus*, he found the link between the conflicting worlds.

CHAPTER VI

RICHARD VON SCHAUKAL. A POET OF AUSTRIA IN DECLINE

To the majority of English students of German literature the name Schaukal conveys little. Even within his own country his work has ceased to be a force in the culture of the nation. Nevertheless, his poetry was for years eagerly read by a small circle in Vienna, where a literary society was founded with the object of spreading interest in his books. His decline in popularity is easily explained. Schaukal has always been a man of rigid artistic integrity and has never been willing to adapt his principles to suit contemporary taste. In consequence much of his work has not been sufficiently in touch with prevailing ideals to awaken interest in a wide public. Furthermore, his range of subjects is narrow, though his output has been prolific.

As the nineteenth century moved to its close and the Viennese school came into prominence, Schaukal's poetry began to be widely read and acclaimed. Thus Rilke dedicated *Traumgekrönt* to him with a quotation from Schaukal's *Verse*. The whole tone of Schaukal's work, with its polished form, its Latin subtlety and its unworldly aestheticism corresponded exactly to the spirit of the age. The outbreak of the war and the disintegration of the social structure with which he felt himself closely linked mark the beginning of his own fall from favour. The troubled years after the Peace and the new orientation of Austrian life and culture engendered in him a bitterness which necessarily left its mark upon his work. He withdrew from public life and, in his days of retirement at Grinzing, sought in the seclusion of his charming home refuge from a world which he felt was crumbling.

Thus it is that much of his work constitutes a strong criticism of his time, and only the greatest poets can be at once the censor and the favourites of their age. Nevertheless, Schaukal has enriched German literature by his exquisite lyrical powers, his gifts as a writer of short stories, his command of the aphorism and, last but not least, by his interpretation of certain greater writers such as E. T. A. Hoffmann and Stifter.

Schaukal's work is a series of fragments of a great confession. Everything that he has published belongs directly or indirectly to this category. He speaks constantly in his work of the days of his childhood, and rarely with greater poignancy than in *Grossmutter. Ein Buch von Tod und Leben* (1906) or *Das Buch Immergrün* (1915). The details of his childhood in Brünn recur throughout his poetry and are always painted with the devotion of one who is homesick for a culture and environment which he knows to be passing away. Here, until his twenty-fifth year, he lived in the Ferdinandgasse, but already by 1918, as we learn from the essays in the volume *Österreichische Züge* (1918), these early memories had become melancholy souvenirs of a lost happiness. Yet they became the inspiration for some of Schaukal's most lasting work, for the many Kinderlieder, for much of *Das Buch der Seele* (1908) and *Die Märchen von Hans Bürgers Kindheit* (1913). A deep consciousness of human evolution as represented by the family unity is evident throughout his work and is mirrored in such poems as "Meinen Kindern" and "Erbe." But it would be mistaken to regard Schaukal as simply a "Heimatdichter," though he clearly has links with that particular phase of German literature called "Heimatkunst." If it were possible to ascribe him to any one movement, it must be to the wider current of neo-romanticism.

Schaukal himself has said that his work falls into three periods; the first ending in 1904, the year following his entry into the Viennese Civil Service, and the second in 1918, when new political circumstances arose which led to his resignation from a share in the administration of the country. These periods make the main stages in his spiritual development.

It is not difficult to discover Schaukal's spiritual masters, and the influences to which he has succumbed reflect in some degree the development of German literature since his birth in 1874. The first two volumes which he published, *Gedichte* (1893) and *Rückkehr. Ein Akt.* (1894), show little originality. They fall within the period when he was under the spell of Heine and Musset. By 1896, when the collection *Verse* appeared, Baudelaire was claiming his attention, and the lyrics in *Meine Gärten. Einsame Verse* (1897) revealed him as moving definitely with the rising tide of neo-romanticism, a follower of the French symbolists and the English Pre-Raphaelites. A journey to England stimulated his enthusiasm for Shakespeare and Keats and deepened the emotional basis of his work. Thus the impressionist style of *Tristia* (1898) and *Tage und Träume* (1899) was more sincere and the artistic touch more assured. His reputation grew. Poems from *Sehnsucht* appeared in the neo-romantic journal *Pan*, and Bierbaum began to interest himself in the young poet. Hoffmann's influence now began to colour his work, and, together with that of Hofmannsthal, left its imprint on *Vorabend* (1902), a one-act play modelled on Hoffmann's story *Der Magnetiseur*. A growing dissatisfaction with the "watery, empty and insincere" art of the symbolists lent a new tone to the story *Mimi Lynx* (1904). This year marked the beginning of a period of great productivity, notable more for its achievements in the sphere of criticism and reflection than for its successes in the realm of creative work.

Since 1900 Schaukal had been writing for the periodical *Gesellschaft*, for the *Literarisches Echo* and the *Wiener Abendpost*, while searching for a new spiritual position. He became increasingly the critic of his time, though he never succeeded completely in detaching himself from its character and its weaknesses. In the *Zettelkasten eines Zeitgenossen* (1913), "Reflections on a period of decline," he adopted the technique of parodying the age in its own terms. The outbreak of the War called forth the *Eherne Sonette* which are more remarkable for their vehemence than for their poetical merit, and the end of the conflict inaugurated a close preoccupation with Hoffmann and those other poets who were to Schaukal, as to so many other writers of the neo-romantic generation, guides, philosophers and friends.

It has been seen in the course of this survey that Schaukal has worshipped at the same shrines as many of his contemporaries. He is above all the poet of neo-romantic ideals, though he is conscious of the weakness and insecurity of many of the principles for which neo-romanticism stood. His poetry bears unmistakably the imprint of neo-romanticism, but, when the neo-romantic ideal succumbed to the wider and more real issues raised by the developments of the War years, he failed to strike his roots in a new spiritual kingdom. Rilke, who grew up in a similar world, was able to broaden and consolidate his art. He passed over into the wider and deeper sphere opened up by the expressionists and beyond that to the consummation of the *Duineser Elegien*. Schaukal, on the other hand, took refuge in criticism.

The scope of his lyrical output is limited. It has not the descriptive resilience of Droste-Hülshoff, for whom Schaukal confesses a deep admiration, nor the fanciful variety of Jean Paul, who appealed irresistibly to the romantic strain in Schaukal's mental make-up. It lacks the emotional appeal of Dehmel, whose poetry Schaukal studied and interpreted and in whom he recognised a kinship of outlook and purpose. Yet, despite its limited range, it is in the lyric that Schaukal has made his most positive contribution.

His life and outlook have been marked by a sense of fearfulness in the face of reality, by an inability to adapt himself to the situation of a changing world. Consequently his lyrics are characterised by a haunting premonition, by a desire to evade the concrete responsibilities of life. It is noteworthy that throughout his work there are but few references to the main social problems of his times. Whereas the general trend of German literature during his lifetime has been in the direction of an increasing consciousness of social responsibility (a tendency to which the expressionists gave a much-needed impetus), Schaukal's development has been towards either negative criticism of his age or preoccupation with his own spiritual problems. In his lyrics there is little merging of individual problems in social or cosmic awareness. Throughout his work we are constantly struck by the words *bang, Bangigkeit, Furcht, Angst*. We notice a persistent search for detachment, as in the poem "Wolken." Sometimes he transfers his own sense of fearful insecurity into the mind of his creations, as in his description of the Hindu girl in "Gefahr" and of the bride in "Der Braut." These poems are found mainly in the earlier collections but those in *Herbsthöhe* reveal the same flinching from reality:

> hinter dem Leben
> halt' ich mich bang.

Everywhere in his work we come across a yearning for detachment from a world in which even the Gospel story of the Resurrection is no lasting consolation ("Auferstehung"), in which purity and happiness are found only in childhood ("Das Neugeborene Kind") and whose temporalness is inseparable from an inborn dualism ("Zeitlichkeit").

Parallel with this feeling of loneliness before a vanished material reality and with the failure to achieve a spiritual synthesis, there is evident in Schaukal's work a search for what may be called a compensating aesthetic reality.

It is enlightening to compare from this point of view the poems in *Herbsthöhe* with those in the earlier volumes. The nature-descriptions belonging to the period of Schaukal's literary début are conceived either derivatively or externally. On the one hand, we find poems such as "An Colombine," which is quite obviously an imitation of Heine, while "Nixe im Wasserfall" and "Persepolis" are merely attempts to recapture the plastic descriptive methods of C. F. Meyer. On the other hand, in these early poems, Schaukal rarely succeeds in depicting Nature except from the standpoint of an observer, as in "Capri." When he aims at merging his personal experiences in his nature-perception, he attains only a superficial stirring of the emotions, such as is illustrated by the poem "Mondenschein."

In his later years Schaukal, however, has revealed new powers as a poet of nature. It is as if the conviction that culture and life have become despiritualised has led him to the desire to find in nature those very qualities which he seeks in vain in existence itself. Thus the poems of the more recent collections show a new conception of nature, which in the meantime has for him become spiritualised, more subtle, more ethereal. Thus in the poem "Lauschend am Eingang," the poet bids his "banished soul" glance into the mysterious tranquillity of nature and there seek peace in "the quiet gardens of days gone by." It would be wrong, however, to suppose that Schaukal's nature-poetry is limited to a sentimental romantic longing. Especially in the later poems he reaches new heights, though his canvas remains unambitious, his art that of the miniaturist. As Professor Nadler has said, Schaukal's most lasting lyrical contribution consists not in its scope but in its rare delicacy. The poem "Geruch der Rose" may serve as an example:

> Geruch der Rose, feinste reichste Garbe
> gesunder selbstverschwiegner Seelengnüge,
> du reinster Hauch geheimnisvoller Züge,
> der Blätterschalen eingestimmter Farbe,
>
> ich beuge mich zu dir, ich schlürfe leise,
> was sich dem zärtlichsten der Sinne schenket,
> selig in geistigsten Genuss versenket,
> und geh' gesättigt von erlesner Speise.

This approach to nature reveals no underlying strength. It is not the confession of a spirit exulting in the joy of life. It is the product of one who has lost the whole world and whose only consolation is the sense of the spiritual beauty of nature's evolution. It is a reflection of Schaukal's personal tragic fate that his best poetry is that in which nature is depicted upon the background of the transience of human life and institutions, and is interfused with a retrospective melancholy. Thus it is that at his best Schaukal makes a real appeal to our craving for sensuous beauty, but he has little to offer us as regards the more pressing problems of existence. We react at once to the aesthetic appeal of such a poem as "Die Libelle":

> Blaublitzende Libelle,
> glanzschwirrend gläserner Schwung,
> stosszuckend auf der Stelle:
> Ursommererinnerung!
>
> Mein Sommer hat hoch im Traume
> des spiegelnden Himmels geschwebt
> und tief im schimmernden Raume
> des Brunnenrundes gebebt.
>
> Er duftete gelb von Rosen,
> farngrün und nelkenrot . . .
> Er schwand mir im Grenzenlosen,
> starb den Libellentod.

But when the poet confesses his own failure and himself proclaims the evasiveness of the reality in which he has put his trust, we cannot wonder that popular esteem has turned rather to the more positive spiritual ideals of his younger Austrian contemporaries such as Josef Weinheber.

Schaukal is essentially the poet of an Austria that no longer exists and, indeed, which ceased to exist immediately after the War. This fact serves largely to explain the general trend and character of his work. His poetry expresses, sometimes powerfully and always poignantly, the fate of a man whose spiritual life was dependent upon the traditions, customs and intellectual background of a vanished order. Like Hofmannsthal, Schaukal feels burdened with the past, with its historical associations and its disappointed hopes:

> Was nicht mehr ist, muss tragen schwer.

He seeks again and again to overcome this sense of burden by rising in his spiritual outlook to a kind of timeless existence in which the mystery of this unintelligible world shall cease to trouble him:

> O wundervolle Kunst, das schwere Leben,
> dem die erliegen, die es bloss erleiden,
> von sich entfernen, ohne es zu meiden,
> sich über es, es zu sich auf zu heben!

This hope is the theme of the poems "Anruf" and "An den Tod," but these moments never represent more than momentary release. Of Schaukal it will be said, as Matthew Arnold said of Wordsworth, that he grew old in an age he condemned, and "the rushing decay of the years that sheltered his youth" undermined his spiritual strength, and thus sapped the vitality of a poet who in more favourable circumstances might well have grown to greater stature.

Chapter VII

LENAU AND BEETHOVEN

The failure of the public for a considerable time to understand the later works of Beethoven is a well-known fact of musical history. It is not, however, generally realised that one of the first people to accept these works with enthusiasm was the poet Nikolaus Lenau (1802–50).

Lenau, or to give him his full name, Nikolaus Franz Niembsch von Strehlenau, was not one of the great minds in German literature; yet he occupies a prominent place in it, largely because of his many lyrical poems and his several epics. Lenau's work and outlook were conditioned very largely by his time. He was to an unusual extent the child of his age.

When Lenau entered upon his studies at the University of Vienna, Austria stood under the influence of Metternich. Metternich was the main figure in the reactionary period that followed on the defeat of Napoleon and the Congress of Vienna, and his influence lay heavily not only on Austria but also on Germany. His determination to stem the rising tide of liberalism led to a strict censorship of the press and of thought generally. The result was that literature in these years was often the expression of a spirit of frustration. Few works are more representative of this period (to which in Germany the name *Biedermeierzeit*[1] is given) than Lenau's epics: *Faust*, 1836,

[1] A good and short account of this period is to be found in the article entitled "Biedermeier" in the Merker-Stammler *Reallexikon*. Those who cannot read German should consult the chapter "German Society in the Reaction" in Prof. Mowat's *The Romantic Age*. Those who wish to probe more deeply into the subject may be referred to the *Deutsche Vierteljahrsschrift*, 1935, Heft 1, which deals *inter alia* with the musical aspect of the period.

Savonarola, 1837, *Die Albigenser*, 1842, or than his lyrics, in particular the *Neuere Gedichte*, 1838–40.

It is clear that for those living at the time of which we are speaking there was little opportunity for active participation in the life of the state, since on all lay the repressive hand of Metternich.[1] Lenau felt these restrictions keenly and in this connection said of his literary works: "My collected works represent my whole life, since I find no opportunity for action." It was in this mood that he turned to music, which by its nature was more able than literature to elude the attentions of the censor. Thwarted in literature, Lenau found consolation and release in the splendid energy of Beethoven, who can be regarded as the greatest exponent of Viennese culture of that time.

Lenau's conception of Beethoven must be examined upon the background also of the German romantics' attitude to music in general. Lenau was not a romantic in the sense that he was a member of the romantic school; indeed his first volume of poems did not appear until 1832, by which time the German romantic school had disappeared. Yet despite the increasing encroachments of realism, romanticism lived on in spirit in Germany and in Austria and in no poet more typically than in Lenau. It is a commonplace of literary criticism to claim that romantic poetry was essentially *musical* in its basis. In German romanticism music had played a fundamental part since the early romantic, Wackenroder, had opened up the path in his *Herzensergiessungen eines kunstliebenden Klosterbruders*.

It is necessary at this point to remember that musical romanticism in Germany differed from the literary movement in two respects. In the first place it was never so well defined and never so centralised within the framework of a "school" as literary romanticism.

[1] There has in recent years been a tendency to take a more lenient view of Metternich and of his régime. Characteristic of this re-orientation is the study by the Austrian historian Srbik.

Schumann recognised that there must be this difference when he said: "It is very hard to believe that in music . . . a special romantic school can be formed." In the second place romanticism in music reached its maturity considerably later than in literature. Thus it was not until *Der Freischütz* of 1821 that it can really be said to have established itself, but by this time literary romanticism was in decline.

Romantic music and poetry meet in E. T. A. Hoffmann, who has been described by Oskar Walzel[1] as the "focus-point of all types of romantic musical experience," and in music Hoffmann finds those qualities which were especially dear to the heart of the German romantics. Thus, talking of Beethoven's *Missa solemnis*[2] he says of romantic music: that it "arouses the feeling of the unknown and the mysterious and the spirit surrenders itself to dreams in which it perceives the supersensual and the infinite." It is important to notice that he regards Beethoven as the representative romantic composer when he says: "Beethoven carries deep down in himself musical romanticism." Although Hoffmann considers Beethoven as a "purely romantic composer" he admits that he still (in 1813) is regarded by many people as a composer who did but "surrender himself blindly to momentary flights of fancy."

Hoffmann and Lenau were among the first appreciative critics of the later works of Beethoven. Hoffmann's approach to Beethoven, however, was very different

---

[1] In his *Deutsche Romantik* (published at Leipzig in the series *Aus Natur- und Geisteswelt*). This has been translated into English, and can be strongly recommended; in one section it deals specifically with the relation between music and poetry in the German romantic movement. The question of Hoffmann's conception of music has been exhaustively examined by C. Schaeffer in his book: *Die Bedeutung des Musikalischen und Akustischen in Hoffmanns literarischem Schaffen*, 1909.

[2] Hoffmann's musical criticisms are to be found mainly in the last section of the collected works, edited by Eduard Grisebach, published at Leipzig.

from that of Lenau.[1] Hoffmann retained some of the exaltation and reverence that were features of early German romanticism; Lenau is coloured by the depression that descended on Austrian and German literature when the period of romanticism had subsided into the straitjacket of the Metternich reaction. The difference in the outlook of these two generations is mirrored in the respective outlook of these two poets on music. Hoffmann proclaimed that for him music was "a song of praise to the Creator," but for Lenau it was the instrument of release from a deep sorrow. Thus we find in his poem, dedicated to the memory of "a beautiful young girl and an able performer of the music of Beethoven," a passage in which Lenau says that in the music of Beethoven he experiences "the sweetness and the harmony of death ":

> Und wie du ins Klavier versunken,
> So träumerisch, so ernst und mild,
> Und wie dem Liede, himmelstrunken,
> Du selber wirst ein schönes Bild;
> Wie dich der grosse Geist umranket,
> Den sie *Beethoven* nannten hie,
> Wie deine zarte Bildung schwanket
> Im Sturme seiner Melodie;
> Der Geist, dem seliges Verderben
> Das Erdenleben sich entlauscht,
> In dessen Lied viel süsses Sterben
> Und Harmonie des Todes rauscht.

In another poem entitled "Beethoven's Bust" Lenau speaks of the "sweet sensation of death" that he finds in Beethoven's works:

> Kämpfen lern' ich ohne Hassen,
> Glühend lieben und entsagen
> Und des Todes Wonneschauer
> Wenn Beethoven's Lieder klagen.

To Max Loewenthal Lenau expressed the opinion that "no one has understood sorrow like Beethoven."

---

[1] Lenau's views on music have been collected by Konrad Huschke in his *Lenau und die Musik*, Regensburg, 1934. Huschke, however, makes no attempt to fit Lenau's views into the background of the period.

Beethoven's music became to Lenau a spiritual necessity and was one of the few rocks in a storm-tossed life. He described it once as a "tonic," and long separation from it caused him acute unhappiness. Thus he wrote to Ludwig August Frankl[1]: "When I do not hear his music for a long period I have a pain in my heart." Beethoven's music was capable of raising him to the highest point of exaltation, but such occasions were inevitably followed by extreme depression. We learn for example from a letter to his friend and biographer Anton Schurz[2] that when Lenau heard "the divine *Fidelio*" for the first time he was "certainly the happiest man on earth"; but this ecstasy had its reaction. "When I reflect on such delights," he said in his letter, "my courage to battle with fate leaves me. Friend, you know Beethoven's music. Beethoven's spirit drove you too like a storm on the rising waves of song, past wild and sublime cliffs, past nocturnal forests and gruesome dungeons; it drove you ever more quickly and more tempestuously until the stream entered a smiling sea of love and joy. God Almighty, what a mind is Beethoven's!" From Frankl we learn that when he was dying Lenau craved to hear the music of Beethoven.

It is regrettable but characteristic that his enthusiasm for Beethoven led him to reject the music of most other composers. He had nothing but contempt for Mozart, who, he said, was to Beethoven as a hill to a mountain. He accused the *Requiem* of hypocrisy and said that serious music was not Mozart's *métier*. He had no respect for Weber and maintained that his best tunes were borrowed from gypsy music. It was only with difficulty and after much persistence that those of his friends who

---

[1] Frankl combined the professions of poetry and medicine and stood in close touch with Lenau. Much valuable information about Lenau is to be found in his book *Zu Lenaus Biographie*, Vienna, 1854.

[2] Cf. *Lenaus Leben, grossentheils aus des Dichters eigenen Briefen. Von seinem Schwestermanne Anton X. Schurz.* Stuttgart & Augsburg, 1855. This has been revised and brought up to date by Castle.

were admirers of Mendelssohn persuaded him to change
his adverse attitude; finally Lenau admitted that he found
the Overture *Die schöne Melusine* moving and spoke
approvingly of *St. Paul*, though he thought it lacked
depth of emotion. He regarded Liszt as a conceited
virtuoso and said that he lacked all qualities of genius.
He rejected Meyerbeer as a musician who was always
striving after effect.

Despite these strong dislikes he found two contemporaries whose music had a strong appeal for him,
Schubert and Zumsteeg, who is known to musical
history mainly on account of his ballads. He once went
so far as to designate the latter as his "favourite" and
praised him especially for his simplicity. He said that
Zumsteeg could be compared with Goethe and Schubert
with Schiller.

Nevertheless, in his opinion Beethoven was the
presiding genius of music. Lenau regarded him with
reverential awe. In the poem on "Beethoven's Bust"
he acknowledged that he respected him as "the greatest
master" and even placed him higher than Shakespeare,
"the great Englishman." It is especially interesting to
observe Lenau's reaction and his pointed references to
those works of Beethoven which he recognised to be
excluded from popular favour at that time. He writes
for instance to the Hofrätin Reinsbeck:

There is scarcely a day which does not bring me some splendid musical
delight. I have for example heard recently the so-called "mad" quartets
of Beethoven. One of them is called the "Devil's Quartet." If the
Devil wrote that, I am his for ever. It has passages at which my heart
nearly burst. Do you know that sweet despair into which Beethoven
carried us?

Lenau attended the first rehearsal of the Ninth
Symphony and found in it "eternal thoughts" and
believed it to be "the greatest work perhaps in all music."

Lenau's approach to Beethoven cannot be classed as
reasoned musical criticism. Of his own work Walzel
could say that it depicted the "spiritual struggles of the

period." He looked at Beethoven through the eyes of an unhappy age, and in his music he found escape from the trammels of his time. He once said that if one is to understand the music of Beethoven "one must be hopelessly in love or otherwise unhappy." Although his interpretation of Beethoven is intensely subjective, it reflects the spiritual longing of the age. Paradoxically he was in advance of his age, for this was the time of which Hoffmann could write: "Beethoven's powerful genius overwhelms the musical masses; they are in vain trying to revolt against it." The interesting fact that emerges from our investigation is that Lenau's importance as a music critic derives not from any critical acumen—he gives us for example no such subtle analysis as his contemporary poet Eduard Mörike gives of Mozart in his delightful short story *Mozart auf der Reise nach Prag*[1]—but from his temperamental identity with his age.

[1] This is now available in a translation by Walter and Catherine Alison Phillips.